Murder & Crime:
Devon

Murder & Crime:
Devon

Mike Holgate

TEMPUS

Frontispiece: 'The Man They Could Not Hang'. John 'Babbacombe' Lee was unwittingly linked to many world-famous crimes and murders of Devon.

First published 2007

Tempus Publishing
Cirencester Road, Chalford,
Stroud, Gloucestershire, GL6 8PE
www.tempus-publishing.com

Tempus Publishing is an imprint of NPI Media Group

British Library Cataloguing in Publication Data.
A catalogue record for this book is available from the British Library.

ISBN 978 0 7524 4504 5

Typesetting and origination by NPI Media Group
Printed in Great Britain

CONTENTS

ACKNOWLEDGEMENTS

The author would like to express his appreciation for access to archive material, books, newspapers and online resources available at the John Pike Local Studies Room, Torquay Central Library.

Illustrations

Supplementing the author's photographic collection, the illustrations in this book have been obtained from contemporary broadsides, song sheets and the following antiquarian magazines and newspapers: *Devon County Standard*, *The Graphic*, *Illustrated London News*, *Illustrated Police News*, *The Penny Illustrated Paper*, *New York Herald*, *Punch*, *The Sphere*, *Sunday Chronicle*, *Torquay Directory & South Devon Journal*.

Poetry

The extracts which appear beneath each chapter heading are verses from Oscar Wilde's Ballad of Reading Gaol (1897).

INTRODUCTION
Criminal Liaisons

While researching the life of Devon's most notorious criminal John 'Babbacombe' Lee, who in 1885 became infamous as 'The Man They Could Not Hang', it emerged that he was inadvertently linked to many other famous crimes: in 1866, Mary Jane Harris, a relative of Lee's had also escaped the death penalty – for infanticide – after turning Queen's evidence against her co-defendant Charlotte Winsor; Kate Farmer, John Lee's fiancée at the time of his arrest for the murder of his employer Emma Keyse, married James Parrish, a seaman who in 1883 had witnessed the shipboard murder of James Carey – a police informer whose evidence had led to the execution of five members of the Irish Invincibles for the assassination of Dublin politicians Thomas Burke and Frederick Cavendish – the son of the Duke of Devonshire; Lee served time alongside gambler Charles Wells, 'The Man Who Broke the Bank at Monte Carlo', who launched his fraudulent 'inventions' in Plymouth and was arrested after fleeing from the port in 1892; Herbert Rowse Armstrong, the Newton Abbot solicitor engaged by Lee's mother to campaign for her son's release, became the only British solicitor to be executed for murder in 1922.

Developing this theme further, Jack-the-Ripper suspect Prince Eddy once met Lee's victim Emma Keyse, whose neighbour Lady Mount-Temple rented her home to Oscar Wilde in 1892. During his stay, an incriminating letter he wrote to his lover Lord Alfred Douglas accelerated the author's downfall. Lady Mount-Temple's nephew, Earl Cowper, Lord Lieutenant of Ireland, was a target for the Irish Invincibles, while her closest friend, Canon Wilberforce, chaplain to the House of Commons, opposed John Lee's impending release from prison by claiming his relatives were, 'a well-known witch family on Dartmoor'.

John Lee eventually gained his freedom 100 years ago in December 1907. He married and had two children before sailing to America with another woman. His deserted wife was forced to seek poor relief in 1912, the year that the *Titanic* sank. At the helm of the ill-fated liner was Robert Hichens. He was one of the fortunate few who survived the disaster and later settled in Torquay where he was arrested for the attempted murder of a business associate in 1933 – the year that John Lee was reported to have died in Milwaukee – yet another intriguing link in the chain of celebrated crimes and murders of Devon.

Mike Holgate

Torquay, *October 2007*

ONE

JACK THE RIPPER:
The Man Who Would be King

For Man's grim Justice goes its way,
And will not swerve aside:
It slays the weak, it slays the strong,
It has a deadly stride:
With iron heel it slays the strong,
The monstrous parricide!

Rumour and innuendo implicate the son and grandson of Queen Victoria with the most mystifying murder cases of her long reign. Outlandish theories suggest that the promiscuous lifestyles of her successor Albert Edward, the Prince of Wales and his eldest son Prince Alfred Victor, the Duke of Clarence, resulted in the respective cover-ups of their lascivious pursuits with the arranged death of a woman in Devon - wrongly attributed to her manservant John 'Babbacombe' Lee, The Man They Could Not Hang' and the mutilation of five London prostitutes by the first serial sex killer Jack the Ripper.

The story began in October 1877, when the Prince of Wales (later Edward VII) accompanied his sons Prince Alfred Victor (known to his family as Prince Eddy) and Prince George (later George V) to Devon. The royal youths were to spend two years on the naval training ship HMS *Britannia* moored on the river Dart between Kingswear and Dartmouth. Their parent's marriage was strained as earlier that year heir apparent Edward had become involved in an illicit affair with married actress Lillie Langtry. Three years previously, the 'Jersey Lily' had visited relatives in Torquay whilst honeymooning on a luxury yacht with her groom Edward Langtry. After living at sea for a year the couple returned to the resort and rented the Villa Engadina for three months. They would remain married in name only after Lillie insisted on moving to the capital where she quickly captivated London society. To many prominent men of the time she was the personification of beauty and everything that was desirable in a woman; artist Millais painted her portrait, politician William Gladstone read poetry to her, aesthetic writer Oscar Wilde slept on her doorstep in homage and the Prince of Wales became her lover.

The Prince and Princess of Wales checked on the progress of their sons when they distributed prizes to naval cadets at Dartmouth in 1878 and a year later, Edward took part in the yacht races at Torbay Regatta. During this visit, he made the short journey to the small fishing community on Babbacombe Beach where he picnicked outside the Cary Arms after renewing his acquaintance with Emma Keyse. During an informal royal visit in 1852, she had personally conducted Edward, his brother Alfred and father Albert the Prince Consort around the grounds of her beach house The Glen, while the head of the royal family, Queen Victoria, remained on board the royal yacht in Babbacombe Bay.

Emma Keyse's mother had nursed the infant Princess Victoria while living at Sidmouth in 1820. The debt-ridden royal family had taken refuge there to escape their London creditors but the visit ended in tragedy when the princess's father, Edward the Duke of Kent suddenly died having contracted pneumonia. Within a week, Victoria's grandfather, 'Mad' King George III was also dead, and with a lack of male heirs, the baby princess took an unwitting step towards eventually claiming the throne in 1837. Four years before this momentous occasion would take place, the fourteen-year-old Princess Victoria, accompanied by her mother the Duchess of Kent, paid a visit to The Glen and took tea with Emma Keyse and her twice-widowed mother Elizabeth Whitehead, who had served the royal family at such a crucial moment in British history.

The royal party prepare to board HMS *Britannia*, 1877.

Emma Keyse was born in 1816, the year that Babbacombe was compared to Babylon by wife murderer Robert Finson who calmly completed his confessional memoirs in the condemned cell while awaiting execution at Exeter Prison. Whilst a sailor on HMS *Namure*, he made the acquaintance of Mary Lear, who came onboard to visit her brother while the ship was anchored in Tor Bay. Despite warnings from his shipmates that her charms had been made readily available to a good many sailors of the fleet, Robert was smitten and avowed to take the girl for his wife. She invited him to stay at her parents' house on Babbacombe Beach, and she wasted no time in making sexual advances towards him while he was accommodated in the spare bedroom. When he returned to sea and sailed to Plymouth he received the news that his intended was pregnant with their child. In his absence, the wedding banns were quickly put up and on his next visit to Torbay, the couple married in November 1801. Finson soon realised his wife was a common prostitute, a profession she readily confessed too, but was to continue to pursue throughout fifteen years of turbulent marriage. She had given birth to an illegitimate child six years earlier, at the age of fifteen, following a fling with the family lodger. Robert Finson doubted whether he was the father of the son born soon after their marriage, but accepted the child as his own. He was certainly not the father of the second of two more children whom his wife conceived while he was imprisoned for six years during the Napoleonic Wars when the vessel in which he was serving was captured. However, his own conduct during this period was little different to that of his wife, as he contracted a dose of the 'pox' after consorting with 'enemy' prostitutes.

Emma Keyse.

Returning home from France after Napoleon's defeat at the Battle of Waterloo, Finson's presence was not welcomed by his wife, nor her father who was of the opinion that only 'gentlemen' of independent means should expect to live in Babbacombe – although his daughter was certainly no lady. For two years, jealousy and hatred grew in Robert Finson's heart as his wife openly conducted affairs in the very house where they lived, having relationships with the tradesman who painted the cottage, the doctor who treated her father's ailments and a continuing relationship with the father of her first-born.

While receiving treatment for a flare-up of his sexually transmitted disease in Exeter, Finson walked to Northernhay to see the county prison where his subsequent violent actions would lead him to end his days. On 6 November 1816, the day before their fifteenth wedding anniversary, the warring Finsons' marriage came to a bloody end. Finson's patience finally snapped, not through his wife's promiscuity, but in an argument over whether their ten-year-old son Robert should be allowed to keep a stray dog he had found. This 'bone' of contention rumbled on for weeks until one morning, Finson brutally chastised his son for allowing the animal in the house. His wife attacked him, 'raging like a mad bull', and cut his face with a hand brush screaming, 'Why don't you kill us all?' The incensed Finson took up the offer and picked up a knife he had spent considerable time sharpening the night before. Time and again he plunged the blade into his spouse, then ran upstairs and stabbed his father-in-law while he lay in bed, before falling on the blade in repeated attempts to commit suicide. Miraculously, Mr Lear survived the attack on his life by his son-in-law, who also staged a remarkable recovery from his self-inflicted wounds.

Four months later Finson stood trial for murder at Exeter Castle. The prisoner's son Robert gave evidence against him, as did his nine-year-old niece Agnes Lane who testified that her uncle had knocked down the victim and stabbed her several times before wiping his bloody hands on the terrified young girl's head. In passing sentence of death, Mr Justice Holroyd concluded that the defendant had, 'given way to an unruly and selfish passion'. The prisoner was executed at the end of March 1817, leaving behind his thoughts on Babbacombe:

> for seduction and other iniquitous proceedings, which are enough to shock the feelings of humanity; it is almost beyond the power of thought or conception to suppose that such a multiplicity of infamy could possibly be exhibited in one house. If I may be allowed to use the expression, it ought to compared to that once great city, Babylon …'

The house of 'infamy' was demolished and another built in its place. In October 1817, it was sold at auction in Exeter after an advertisement in *The Times* glossed over recent events, describing the new abode at the scene of the crime as, 'a Marine Cottage, lately erected, possessing all the requisites for cheerful and elegant retirement'. By 1830 it belonged to the parents of Emma Keyse. She, too, was to become the victim of yet another 'Babbacombe Murder' – committed, it was whispered, because the puritanical spinster had voiced her disapproval of the scandalous affair between Edward and Lillie. Therefore, she was silenced because her royal connections believed she 'knew too much'. The victim received her last royal visit when the Prince and Princess of Wales took their sons Eddy and George to Babbacombe in 1880. The royal party generously handed out half-sovereigns to each of the household servants of Miss Keyse. The youngest of these was the cook Amelia Lee, whose brother John had recently left the household to join a naval training vessel at Plymouth. He was subsequently invalided out of the service with pneumonia, and a few months after returning to The Glen in 1884 was convicted of the seemingly senseless killing of his elderly employer Miss Keyse (see Chapter 2). Prince Eddy would be suspected of carrying out the Whitechapel murders in 1888 – the year that Rudyard

Kipling, educated at Westward Ho! and one-time resident of Torquay, wrote about the rise and fall of 'The Man Who Would Be King'. Murder suspects John Lee and Prince Eddy were from very different backgrounds but shared the same birth year – 1864. While Prince Eddy had all the privileges of a royal upbringing with the expectation that one day he would succeed his father and be crowned king, John Lee was the son of a poor clay miner from Abbotskerswell, near Newton Abbot, who longed only for a life at sea. The prince, like the pauper, would fail to achieve his goal due to a bout of pneumonia.

According to one Ripper theory, Prince Eddy was a syphilitic who, in his madness, went on the rampage eliminating women engaged in the world's oldest profession from whom he had contracted the then incurable disease. Court records, however, give Prince Eddy convincing alibis for his whereabouts when the killer struck and some Ripper theorists have attributed the Whitechapel murders to people acting in his interests. According to one version, eminent artist Walter Sickert had a studio in Cleveland Street that was regularly visited by Prince Eddy. The prince fell in love with a girl called Annie Crook who worked in a nearby tobacconist's shop. The couple were secretly married and had a baby daughter named Alice. The Establishment were horrified when they learned of the young royal's involvement with a commoner. Early in 1888, Prince Eddy was sent abroad and in his absence his unsuitable 'wife' was forcibly committed to an asylum. Their child had been left in the care of Annie's friend Mary Jane Kelly,

The Glen (centre), Babbacombe Beach, 1830.

John Lee.

who had witnessed the marriage and now feared for her life at the hands of the authorities. Leaving the child with Walter Sickert, she took refuge in the East End, where she confided in three female friends and together they hatched a plot to blackmail the Government. Faced with the prospect of a scandal which could bring down the royal family, the Prime Minister, Lord Salisbury, enlisted the help of the Freemasons. They in turn arranged for Queen Victoria's physician Sir William Gull to butcher the women, making the attacks look like the work of a madman. He was ably assisted by Walter Sickert, who acted as lookout, and John Netley, a coachman who had frequently conveyed Prince Eddy to Cleveland Street. One by one, Gull started to eliminate Kelly's friends. On 31 August, the mutilated body of Mary 'Polly' Nichols was found. Unable to afford a bed in a lodging house, she had been trying to raise money by prostitution when her throat was cut right through to the spinal column before her skirts were raised and her abdomen ripped open exposing her intestines. A week later Annie Chapman met a similar fate, except that her intestines were removed and laid neatly on the ground, while her womb was removed and taken away by her killer. At the end of September, two women were slain in a single night. Elizabeth Stride was last seen talking to a man 'respectable' in appearance, less than thirty minutes before her body was discovered. This time there was no mutilation and blood was still seeping from the wound in the victim's throat, indicating that the Ripper had narrowly escaped detection. Forty minutes later, Gull thought that he had completed his grim task when he slashed the throat and stomach of Katherine Eddowes, also known by the alias Mary Ann Kelly. With maniacal zeal her throat, face and abdomen were slashed and a kidney and womb removed. Having mistaken the victim for blackmailer Mary Jane Kelly, the deadly trio took to the streets once more and finally located their target on 9 November 1888. When a rent collector called on Kelly he found her naked, bloodied corpse lying on the bed. Her face had been slashed almost beyond recognition; flesh removed from her abdomen and thighs was

Above: Ceremony installing Prince Eddy as a grandmaster of the Freemasons – the organisation said to have to have arranged the Whitechapel Murders.

Right: Kate Eddowes was killed in error.

found on a bedside table, while the breasts had been cut off and her heart extracted and removed from the scene of the crime.

The vital witness to the marital indiscretion of Prince Eddy had been silenced but two years later, his royal highness was involved in another scandal in Cleveland Street, when a number of his aristocratic friends were arrested during a police raid on a male brothel where they engaged in sex acts with rent boys. One of those apprehended was Lord Arthur Somerset who escaped prosecution when he threatened to implicate Prince Eddy in the matter unless he was allowed to slip away into exile. Prince Eddy's sexuality had long been the subject of conjecture which, in the wake of the 'rent-boy' scandal, he attempted to overcome by contemplating marriage to his French cousin Princess Helene d'Orleans, which precipitated a constitutional crisis as she was a Catholic.

The British press suppressed criticism of the royals, but correspondents found willing recipients for their sensational stories abroad. *The American Daily Northwestern* published this damning indictment of Prince Eddy and the bad example set by his father Prince Edward in 1890:

> Cable reports from England announce that Prince Victor Albert, eldest son of the Prince of Wales and heir presumptive to the throne, has returned from India, where he had gone to escape the smoke

Prince Eddy: inherited 'his father's vices without retaining many of his virtues'.

of the Cleveland street scandal, in which he was mixed up. The information is further vouchsafed that Prince Victor insists on marrying his cousin against the protests of the royal house, and offers to renounce his claims to the throne in favour of his next younger brother, George, if he is allowed to marry the girl of his choice and have a satisfactory competency settled upon him. It is hinted that the people generally would prefer to see the wild young prince accommodated in his freak, for the reason that physically and mentally he is something of a wreck and not half the man in all the attributes of a manly makeup that characterise George. Victor seems to inherit his father's vices without retaining many of his virtues, and his connections with the Cleveland street scandal is only another indication of the debauchery which too conspicuously punctures European royalty. The inbred crowd of royal stock of all Europe is becoming sadly deteriorated both bodily and mentally, and cannot long, in any event, survive the strength of a higher order of governmental civilization which the common people are attaining. Whether England will ever have a king after the Prince of Wales is a matter of speculation, and some prophets have gone so far as to predict that England will never have another king.

Despite the sullied reputations of two princes of the realm, the monarchy survived when the Prince of Wales succeeded his mother Queen Victoria in 1901, to be followed by Prince George

Edward, the Prince of Wales.

Left: Robert James Lees.

Opposite: The Ripper strikes again!

in 1910, Prince Albert Victor having passed away aged only twenty-seven in 1892. The official cause of death was pneumonia although there has been speculation that this was a by-product of syphilis, bringing about a premature end to an iniquitous life.

The death of Sir William Gull had been announced in 1890, although it is contended that he had in fact been secretly incarcerated in an asylum when his role as Jack the Ripper had been uncovered by the police acting on information from a well-known former journalist and medium Robert James Lees. Although the name of the suspect was not mentioned, there were many clues to his identity in the story broken by the *Chicago Sunday Times-Herald*, 28 April 1895:

Robert James Lees, the gentleman to whom the unfortunate of the east end of London owe their present immunity from the attacks of a monster who for long years made every one of them venture out at night literally with her life in her hands, is the person entitled to the credit of tracking Jack the Ripper ... In his early years Mr Lees developed an extraordinary clairvoyant power, which enabled him to discern, as with the eyes of a seer, things hidden from the comprehension of ordinary men born without this singular gift. At the age of 19 he was summoned before the Queen at Birmingham, and he gave evidence of his powers as a clairvoyant which excited her majesty's utmost astonishment. Having considerable means of his own, however, he devoted himself to literary pursuits, became a profound theologian and ultimately took up the study of spiritualism and theosophy. He is at present the recognised leader of the Christian Spiritualists in Great Britain.

At the time of the first three murders by the ripper, Mr Lees was in the height of his clairvoyant powers. One day he was writing in his study when he became convinced that the ripper was about

to commit another murder. He tried in vain to dispel the feeling. As he sat at his table the whole scene arose before him … Such was the extraordinary clairvoyant vision presented to the second sight of Mr Lees. So impressed was he by what he had thus miraculously witnessed, that he at once went to Scotland Yard and detailed the whole matter to the detectives. As they regarded him as nothing short of a lunatic, and had been for some months visited by all sorts and conditions of cranks with Jack-the-Ripper theories, he naturally received little attention …

One day, while riding in an omnibus from Shepherd's Bush in company with his wife, he experienced a renewal of the strange sensations which had preceded his former clairvoyant condition. The omnibus ascended Notting Hill. It stopped at the top, and a man entered the interior of the vehicle. Mr Lees at once experienced a singular sensation. Looking up he perceived that the new passenger was a man of medium size. He noticed that he was dressed in a dark suit of Scotch tweed, over which he wore a light overcoat. He had a soft felt hat on his head.

Over a year had elapsed since Mr Lees' clairvoyant vision, but the picture of the murderer had been indelibly impressed upon his mind. Leaning over to his wife he remarked earnestly, 'That is Jack the Ripper,' his wife laughed at this, and told him not to be foolish. 'I am not mistaken,' replied Mr Lees, 'I feel it.' The omnibus traversed the entire length of the Edgware road, turning into Oxford street at the marble arch. At this point the man in the light overcoat got out.

Mr Lees determined to follow him. Bidding his wife continue on her journey in the direction of home, he followed the man down Park lane. About half way down the thoroughfare he met a constable, to whom he pointed out the man in the light overcoat informing him that he was the dreaded 'ripper' and asking that he be arrested. The constable laughed at him, and threatened to 'run him in.' It seems that the 'ripper' must have entertained some apprehension that he was in danger, for on reaching Apsley House he jumped into a cab and was driven rapidly down Piccadilly. A minute later Mr Lees met a police sergeant to whom he confided his suspicions. 'Show me the constable who refused to arrest him!' exclaimed the sergeant. 'Why it was only this morning that we received news at the Bow Street station that the 'ripper' was coming in this direction.' …

Mr Lees hastened to Scotland Yard, where he insisted on having an immediate audience with the head inspector of police … The inspector himself, who was a religious man … seemed to recognise in Mr Lees an instrument of providence – and he determined then and there to avail himself of his marvellous, though altogether incomprehensible powers.

After an earnest appeal from the inspector, Mr Lees consented to try and track the 'Ripper' – much in the same way as a bloodhound pursues a criminal. There seemed to be some magnetic wave connecting an impalpable sense he possessed with the fugitive. All that night Mr Lees submitted himself to his strange magnetic influence and traversed swiftly the streets of London. The inspector and his aids followed a few feet behind him. At last, at 4 o'clock in the morning, with pale face and bloodshot eyes, the human bloodhound halted at the gates of a west end mansion, gasping with cracked and swollen lips, as he pointed to an upper chamber where a faint light yet gleamed.

'There is the murderer – the man you are looking for.'

'It is impossible,' returned the inspector. 'That is the residence of one of the most celebrated physicians in the west end.' … [Finally convinced] the inspector caused a thorough search of the house to be made, when ample proofs were found that the doctor was the murderer. Among others

Sir William Gull identified by Robert James Lees as 'Jack the Ripper'.

the detectives brought to light the famous Scotch tweed suit and soft felt hat, together with the light overcoat. When convinced of his guilt, the unfortunate physician begged them to kill him at once, as he 'could not live under the same roof with such a monster.'... He was at once removed to a private insane asylum in Islington, and he is now the most intractable and dangerous madman confined in that establishment.

In order to account for the disappearance of the doctor from society a sham death and burial were gone through, and an empty coffin, which now reposes in the family vaults in Kensal Green, is supposed to contain the mortal remains of a great west end physician, whose untimely death all London mourned.

The source of this story was believed to be Lees' close friend, William Stead, the world's best known journalist, who was to lose his life on the *Titanic* [see Chapter 7]. Within weeks of this sensational revelation, Lees closed down the People's League – a successful benevolent society which aided the poor. Its founder curiously left London for 'health reasons' although he was to survive another thirty-six years after moving to the West Country. His spiritualist friends later indicated that he had been granted a royal pension and advised to relocate to avoid press attention. After living in St Ives for five years, he moved to Plymouth in 1900 where he became honorary pastor at a chapel in Plymouth – oddly, the only non-conformist chapel ever to be endowed by Queen Victoria. From 1902 until 1928, Lees made his home in Ilfracombe and concentrated on writing novels with the aid of his 'spirit guide'. His healing powers made the news in 1923 when he 'cured' a girl at a meeting of the Paignton Spiritualist Society. Leonora Pethybridge had been certified insane and institutionalised for eight years after attempting to starve herself (the patient was probably suffering from anorexia nervosa, a condition first identified by Dr William Gull). She was released in order to meet Lees who emerged victorious after a two-hour 'battle' and the girl was allowed home to continue a normal existence.

In 1931, Lees passed away at the age of eighty-one, having spent the last two years of his life in his native Leicester. His ashes were interred alongside those of his spouse who had pre-deceased him in Ilfracombe. His death left many queries unanswered. There is only circumstantial evidence to prove any connection with the celebrated murder case. Lees and his family of sixteen children suffered severe financial hardship for many years prior to 1889; his fortunes were mysteriously restored just months after the last of the Whitechapel murders. In addition to the alleged pension from the privy purse, it is claimed that he received a substantial reward for apprehending Jack the Ripper. This windfall enabled him to set up his own philanthropic mission which, was suddenly abandoned after the newspaper article citing his involvement in the murder investigation appeared in Chicago in 1895. Lees' obituary revealed that he had spoken to the press on the matter for the first time shortly before his death without confirming the suspect's name which he took beyond the grave:

Mr Robert James Lees ... claimed to be the only surviving person who knew the identity of Jack the Ripper ... Some months ago, he told a Leicester Mercury man that he offered his services to Scotland Yard, with a view to tracing the criminal. ... Mr Lees made the astounding statement ... that he actually enabled the Yard to associate with the crime, a man who died in a lunatic asylum.

(*Leicester Mercury*, 12 January 1931)

TWO

JOHN LEE:
The Man They Could Not Hang

He lay as one who lies and dreams
In a pleasant meadow-land,
The watcher watched him as he slept,
And could not understand
How one could sleep so sweet a sleep
With a hangman close at hand?

The village of Babbicombe [an early derivation of the place-name Babbacombe] situated on the shore of a small bay on the south Devon coast, between Teignmouth and Torquay, was the scene of a cruel murder perpetrated on Saturday 15 inst. An elderly maiden lady, Miss Emma Keyse, sixty-eight years of age, resided in a pretty marine villa at the foot of the cliff, surrounded by wooded pleasure-grounds, which is called The Glen. She is said to have dwelt there more than forty years. The house [which is shown in our illustration overleaf] was a low thatched building, but sufficiently commodious; and Miss Keyse, living there with none of her family or friends, often entertained visitors and private yachting parties. She kept three female servants, one of whom had a half-brother, John Lee, twenty years old, and he was the butler in Miss Keyse's household. In the night, or between 3 and 4 a.m., the cook smelt burning, and gave the alarm. It was discovered that the house had been set on fire in three places: in the drawing-room, in the dining room, and in Miss Keyse's bedroom. The dead body of the unfortunate lady was found in the dining room, with a deep gash across the throat, and with the side of the head smashed, as by a blow with some heavy instrument. No one had broken into the house. John Lee, whose behaviour and appearance at the time seemed very suspicious, is charged with the murder. His previous character was bad, as he underwent six months' imprisonment for stealing a plate from a former master; and he was under notice to quit the service of Miss Keyse.

The Glen: scene of the Babbacombe Murder.

Shocked members of society learned of the 'The Murder at Babbicombe' when the above report appeared in the *Illustrated London News* in November 1884. John Lee, the servant charged with the appalling crime was raised in the village of Abbotskerswell situated midway between Torquay and the market town of Newton Abbot. Born in 1864, the second child of John and Mary, he attended the village school with his sister Amelia who was two years older. The children also had an elder half-sister, Elizabeth Harris, the illegitimate daughter of their mother, who was cared for by her grandparents in the nearby village of Kingsteignton. All three children, known to the family as Jack, Millie and Lizzie, would at some point find employment in the service of Emma Keyse, who had inherited The Glen upon the death of her mother in 1871.

The murder suspect had joined the household of The Glen in 1878, then left two years later to join the Royal Navy. Stationed at Devonport on the training ship HMS *Implacable* he was awarded 'first prize for general progress' then forced to relinquish his naval career on health grounds following a serious bout of pneumonia. Returning to south Devon in January 1882, he obtained a position as 'boots' – cleaning the footwear of guests at the Yacht Club Hotel, Kingswear. Dissatisfied with this lowly occupation, he gained employment as a porter at Kingswear Railway Station, then, a month later, early in October, was transferred to the goods department at Torre Station, Torquay. He later recalled in his autobiography how he had only been there one week when fate intervened in the shape of his former employer Emma Keyse who presented him with a golden opportunity to further his prospects by arranging for him to work as a footman in the service of Colonel Brownlow, of Ridgehill, Torquay. However, six months later the young servant was apprehended in Devonport attempting to pawn the family silver whilst the Brownlows were holidaying abroad. Victorian courts took a dim view of

John Lee.

servants transgressing against their masters and a custodial sentence was the predictable outcome of Lee's trial held in July 1883 at Exeter Assizes.

Given a 'lenient' sentence of six months' imprisonment with hard labour at Exeter Prison, having already spent three months remanded in custody awaiting trial, Lee's future prospects as a convicted felon looked decidedly grim until he was offered yet another lifeline by Emma Keyse, whom he had let down badly after she had recommended him to Colonel Brownlow. Despite this breach of trust, she evidently still thought well of Lee, believing he had simply been 'led astray'. On New Year's Day 1884, shortly before Lee's imminent release, her letter to the governor was passed to the prison chaplain, the Reverend John Pitkin, with an offer which would enable the prisoner to rebuild his life and gain a 'character' reference:

Sir, I hope you will excuse my troubling you, but I feel anxious to know what report you can give me of John Lee? Whether he has conducted himself satisfactorily, and whether those who have had much to do with him can give a good report, and whether you consider that he truly and really feels the great sin he has been led into, and whether he is really penitent. I shall be grateful, if you will make careful enquiries, in addition to your own personal opinion. He lived with me as a lad, and I liked him very much, and found him very honest and truthful and obedient. I had no particular fault to find with him, but considered his was a simple-minded, easy disposition that would be easily led astray, and hoped, by being on a training-ship, he would gain stability of character and purpose, and was very sorry that his health would not admit of his remaining. I feel much interested in his family and himself; and have told his mother that I will take him back into my service, and to work in the garden with my gardener for a while, to be able to give him a character, until something desirable may turn up.

John Lee accepted the opportunity to work temporarily for a token wage whilst Miss Keyse attempted to find him gainful employment elsewhere and give him a fresh start in life. His gratitude was short-lived however, for prospective employers, mindful of the unpleasant experience of Colonel Brownlow, were not easily persuaded by Miss Keyse's pleas to, 'give the poor boy another chance'. As the months went by, Lee became argumentative and disrespectful through what he perceived to be her failure to find him a suitable position. He began to refer to her in derogatory terms as 'the old woman'. It was as if he began to blame the elderly lady for the hopelessness of the position his crime had placed him in. The situation was exacerbated when he became engaged to Kate Farmer as he was not earning enough to support a wife. Friction within The Glen continued to mount further when Miss Keyse, who had been trying to sell her estate for some considerable time, succeeded in finding a buyer for the property at an auction conducted in London on 28 October. Later that day, she paid the servants their quarterly salaries, owed in arrears, and Lee was bitterly upset to learn that she had reduced his wages from half a crown to the miserly sum of 2s a week. Tragically, his employer was killed a little over two weeks after reassuring Lee that she would try and persuade the new owners to keep him on. Suspicion for her brutal murder quickly fell upon 'the only man in the house'.

During the subsequent Inquest, Magistrates Hearing and Murder Trial, Lee was not required to venture any information about what happened that fateful night. It was not until many years later when he sold his 'life-story' to a newspaper that the public eventually got the opportunity to hear his version of events:

And so I come to November 14, 1884. The first thing I distinctly remember is seeing my step-sister, Elizabeth Harris [who had replaced her half-sister Amelia Lee as cook at The Glen], going to her bedroom. It was teatime. As she looked queer I asked her what was the matter. She said she didn't feel well. 'Shall I fetch Dr. Chilcote?' I said. She replied, rather shortly I thought, 'Oh, no, no!'

I was afterwards told that she was in bed. At all events, I did not see her for the rest of that day.

At seven o'clock I went to the post, as was my duty every day. Then I went round to see Miss Farmer, and at ten o'clock I returned to 'The Glen.' After supper I went in to prayers with Eliza and Jane Neck [elderly sisters who had served the family for some forty years]. Miss Keyse said the prayers. It was always a touching little service. I shall never forget the picture – old Miss Keyse reading the prayers and a chapter from the bible.

In a quarter of an hour the prayers were said, and at eleven o'clock I went to bed in the pantry. The other two servants didn't go just then. Jane was in the pantry putting away some things. She used to go about her work, although I was asleep, or, perhaps, getting into bed. She never worried about me. Miss Keyse never used to go to bed till one or two o'clock in the morning. I think Jane Neck stayed up for about half-an-hour. The last thing she did was to put a nib of cocoa on the kitchen hob for our mistress. This was done every night. Miss Keyse used to go into the kitchen herself and carry the cocoa up to her bedroom. On this particular night I think I was asleep before Jane had finished. But I do know that Miss Keyse had told Jane to tell me that there was a note in the pantry for me to take to Colonel McLean's [Miss Keyse's brother-in-law] in the morning, with a brace of pheasants. Miss Keyse often left notes like that, and I attended to them in the morning.

The next thing I remember is being roused up before daybreak by my step-sister shouting 'Fire! Fire!' I jumped out of bed and put on my shirt, socks, and trousers. At the top of the stairs I saw the three women. The house was full of smoke. Eliza Neck was shouting: 'Where's Miss Keyse? Where's Miss Keyse?'

We rushed into Miss Keyse's bedroom. The old lady was not there. Terror-stricken, Eliza Neck went running about the rooms upstairs, but there was no sign of Miss Keyse. I could see flames

FINDING THE BODY OF MISS KEYSE

The smouldering body of the victim is discovered by the household servants.

coming out of my mistress's room, and also out of another room. Eliza was the first to go into the dining-room. Jane and I waited outside. The smoke was so thick that I could hardly see her. I heard Jane call out, 'We shall all be stifled!'

Realising the danger I rushed headlong into the dining-room in order to open the windows. I tried to open the French window on the right, but I couldn't. So I pushed my arm through the glass. I cut my arm and left a bit of flesh on the pane. I could feel the blood pouring down my sleeve and soaking it. But what did it matter?

I little thought that afterwards my fate would practically turn on that trivial circumstance. The smoke was now pouring out of the room, and we looked about us. 'Oh! Where is Miss Keyse?' I heard one of the women say. As she spoke I looked round. My mind recoils with horror as I think of it. There spread before me, was the answer to my cry. My poor dear mistress was lying on the carpet

The arrest of John Lee.

- a ghastly sight. I can see her eyes staring out from the hair which had fallen about her face. I can still see her hands. They were blue and 'clawlike' - drawn up in convulsions of death. I just took one glance at the body and went out.

Jane and I at once called a man named Stiggins, who was living in one of Miss Keyse's cottages on the beach. He was a fisherman. Then I went back to the house. I remember that we also called Mr. Gaskin, the landlord of the Cary Arms. Several other people came as well. I went back to the dining-room. The smoke had now gone. Miss Keyse was lying by the sofa. There was blood on her throat. The body looked as if an attempt had been made to burn it, but I did not notice any paper about or oil. With the assistance of Mr. Gaskin I carried the body outside. Nearly all the clothes had been burnt off it, Mr. Gaskin lifted her by the head, and I took her by the feet.

Next I remember that I went back into the dining-room, and helped to put out the fire. The people in the house wanted someone to go and break the news to Colonel McLean. I was sent. I ran all the way to the house in Torquay, and threw some gravel up at the servant's window. After the gravel had been rattling against the panes for several moments the window was thrown up and a servant put out her head. 'There's been a fire at Miss Keyse's,' I said. 'Tell Mrs. McLean [the victim's sister] I want her'.

I was admitted into the hall, and presently I saw Mrs. McLean standing on top of the landing. 'Miss Keyse's place has been on fire,' I told her, 'and the poor old lady is badly burnt.' On my way back to 'The Glen' I met the chimney sweep. I think I also called a policeman.

At the trial something was said about an axe. It is quite true that I was asked for one when they were putting out the fire. They wanted to chop down a beam. I went out to the woodhouse and got the axe I knew would be there.

How quickly that terrible morning passed! Still less did I pause to recollect that on the night before the tragedy, I was the only man in the house!

As soon as things got a bit quiet I wanted to go to the doctor to get my arm dressed. By that time my shirt was soaked with blood. At the door of 'The Glen' there was a policeman, I told him where I was going. Holding up a hand he said: 'You can't go there alone. I must go with you.' I protested strongly against such absurd treatment. The real meaning of it did not dawn on me. However, the policeman went to the superintendent, and asked him if he was to go with me to the surgery. 'No,' said the superintendent. 'Let him go himself.'

After my arm had been dressed I went back to the house, and sat down with the firemen in the kitchen. Suddenly the superintendent called me to him. 'Lee,' he said, 'you will be apprehended on suspicion.' I said, 'On suspicion? - Oh!' I was too astonished to say anything else. He answered, 'You are the only man in the house!' Almost dazed, I was handed over to the sergeant. I could hardly speak. I could not think. My tongue was tied. As I was going through my step-sister, Elizabeth Harris, said to me: 'Where are you going to?' I said, 'I am taken on suspicion.' She answered, 'I know you didn't do it!'

As I left the house for Torquay police-station I heard Mr. Gaskin say that 'something foul' had been done. That is all I know about the murder of Miss Keyse. I take Almighty God as my judge - I have spoken the truth. Miss Keyse was my best friend.

Despite his plea of innocence, the evidence against Lee, though circumstantial, was considerable. The victim had been attacked in the hall and her manservant claimed he heard nothing as he slept less than 3m away on a fold-down bed in the pantry. A can of paraffin used to set fire to the body and the house had been stored in the pantry where an intruder would have had to climb over Lee's bed to reach it then put it back. The weapons used to bludgeon the skull and cut the throat of the victim were said to be an axe produced by Lee to fight the fire and a bloodied knife found in a drawer in the pantry leading the police to the obvious conclusion of who was the guilty party. When the case came to trial, the jury took only forty minutes to deliver a verdict of guilty to the court at Exeter Castle. Donning the black cap to pass sentence of death Judge Manisty pronounced:

John Lee you have been found guilty of a crime as barbarous as was ever committed, and this jury have found you guilty of the murder upon evidence so clear to my mind, and so absolutely conclusive, that I am sorry to say I cannot entertain a doubt of the correctness of their verdict. You say you are innocent; I wish I could believe it. You have throughout the case maintained a calm appearance, but I need not say the jury having found you guilty of the crime of this murder, I am not surprised to see you maintain such a calm appearance.

The crowded courtroom was astonished when the defendant boldly replied, 'My lord, the reason I am so calm is because I trust in my Lord, who knows I am innocent'.

Of the thirty witnesses who were called by the prosecution at the trial of John Lee, the most damning evidence against the suspect was delivered by his half-sister Elizabeth Harris. She gave details of frequent 'threats' he had uttered against his employer. When given notice to leave her service he had said that if Miss Keyse did not give him a character reference he would, 'level the place to ashes' On another occasion when she had been grumbling about his work, he pronounced that if she had been near a cliff, he would have, 'pushed her over'. When his poor wage was reduced he reiterated that he would have his revenge by, 'setting the house on fire and going up on the hill to look at it'. These allegations caused a sensation in court. However,

The Cook, Elizabeth Harris (half sister of John Lee.)

Elizabeth Harris.

Elizabeth Harris's 'character' was also questionable for she was in the early stages of pregnancy at the time of the murder. Defence counsel failed to ask her who the father of her child was, but suggested, in an half-hearted summing-up, that her unknown lover might well have visited her on the night in question and reacted violently when discovered leaving the house by the victim. From the condemned cell, John Lee made it clear that Elizabeth was responsible for his plight in a letter to his sister Amelia, 'Don't blame Lizzie, I do not blame her, I should have opened my mouth before'.

Elizabeth Harris had been raised by her maternal grandmother Betsy Harris and her second husband William Stevens. Coincidentally, Betsy had been called to give evidence against another family member, her niece Mary Jane Harris, who stood trial for murder in 1865. Mary Jane, the cousin of John Lee's mother, was a servant in Torquay and had a seven-year relationship with a Farmer Nickells. She bore him two children. What became of the eldest was never disclosed, but the lifeless body of the second child named Thomas was found dumped in a lane wrapped in newspaper in February 1865.

Mary Jane Harris and her childminder Charlotte Winsor were indicted for infanticide. When first questioned by the police, the pair claimed that two-month-old Thomas was alive and well and being cared for by Betsy Stevens. However, Mary Jane's aunt was totally unaware that her niece had even been expecting a baby. The only child in her charge was her seven-year-old grandchild Elizabeth Harris, daughter of Mary Lee, née Harris, who had fallen pregnant out of wedlock while working on a farm at Widecombe.

Charlotte Winsor was a witch-like figure who believed she was 'doing good' by disposing of unwanted children. The 'baby-farmer' had smothered Thomas Harris, in his mother's presence, but at the first trial held at Exeter Castle, the jury failed to reach a verdict on how to apportion blame for the baby's death. At the retrial, Mary Jane Harris was persuaded to save her own neck by the prosecution and released after turning Queen's evidence against Winsor who

Charlotte Winsor and the house where she killed baby Thomas Harris.

was sentenced to death. On two occasions hangman William Calcraft was thwarted when the prisoner was granted a late stay of execution then, a reprieve. She was obliged to remain in prison until her death in 1894. At the first appointed execution of the notorious 'baby farmer', a souvenir broadsheet was published in advance of the capital punishment which did not take place:

> At the usual hour this morning Mrs Winsor expiated her crime on the gallows. Thousands assembled in front of the gaol at a very early hour, and many had walked all night to see the execution. Great commotion prevailed and it was evident that the crowd viewed the execution of a woman as a novelty, while they freely discussed the fiendish nature of the culprit, and expressed their total abhorrence of one who could make a business of murdering illegitimate offsprings.

Similarly, some twenty years later, a totally inaccurate report of an intended execution appeared prematurely in an early edition of the *Dartmouth & Brixham Chronicle*, 'The condemned man John Lee was executed at Exeter this morning. … The culprit died easily'.

The editor was deeply embarrassed when his assumption of the condemned man's death proved to be somewhat exaggerated, for, on the morning of Monday 23 February 1885, as the bell at Exeter Prison tolled the death knell for John Lee, anxious officials assembled nervously on the scaffold. It was their painful duty to witness the execution and more than one had fortified himself with a drop of Dutch courage, although nothing could have prepared them for the harrowing scenes that were to follow.

The executioner, James Berry, quickly pinioned the condemned man, drew a white cap over his head and then tightened the noose around his neck.

'Have you anything to say?' he whispered.

'No', came the firm reply, 'Drop away'!

Execution of Mrs. Winsor

At Exeter,
For the barbarous murder of Mary Jane Harris's Child

A premature report of the death of Charlotte Winsor.

The hangman hesitated while the prison chaplain concluded the service from the Burial of the Dead, 'Now is the Christ risen from the dead ... '

At the appropriate moment, Berry pulled a lever to activate the 'drop', then gasped in amazement as the trap door merely sagged 2in, leaving the prisoner precariously suspended between life and death!

'Quick stamp on it', he shouted to the warders.

Distressing scenes followed as desperate efforts were made to force the trap open. Warders virtually jumped on the doors and risked falling into the pit with the prisoner had they been successful, but after several minutes the bewildered prisoner was led to one side, while the apparatus was tested and found to work perfectly. Visibly shaken, Berry made a second attempt, but to no avail. Heaving with all his might, he succeeded only in bending the lever.

'This is terrible', cried the anguished governor. 'Take the prisoner away!'

An artisan warder was summoned to diagnose the problem and a saw passed around the frame of the trapdoors to relieve possible pressure on the wooden boards, swollen by overnight rain. Satisfied that the fault had now been remedied, the governor recalled the prisoner to face his ordeal for a third time. The witnesses were in a great state of shock and the chaplain trembled as he read a passage from the service, 'The last enemy to be destroyed is death.'

Perspiring freely, Berry grasped the lever with both hands, determined that this time, John Lee would keep his appointment in Hell! The bolt was drawn and the scaffold shuddered.

'Is it all over?' pleaded the chaplain, afraid to look.

'In God's name, put a stop to this!' exclaimed Mr Caird, the surgeon. 'You may experiment as much as you like on a sack of flour, but you shall not experiment on this man any longer'.

The attempted execution of 'The Man They Could Not Hang'.

The Reverend Pitkin opened his eyes and almost collapsed when he realised that Lee had survived a third attempt on his life. He immediately informed the under-sheriff, Henry James, 'I cannot carry on!'

Without the presence of a chaplin to sign the death certificate, the execution could not continue, therefore it was agreed to postpone the proceedings pending instructions from the Home Secretary.

John Lee was returned to his cell, seemingly unaffected by his torment, but reacted angrily when Berry came in to remove his bonds.

'Don't do that', he protested, 'I want to be hung!'

'Have no fear', reassured the chaplain, with tears in his eyes, 'By the laws of England they cannot put you on the scaffold again!'

Lee recovered his composure, then suddenly recalled an extraordinary occurrence, which he had recounted earlier that morning to two warders, 'I saw it all in a dream! I was led down to the scaffold and it would not work – after three attempts, they brought me back to my cell!'

The Reverend Pitkin's assurance to Lee that he was legally protected from having to face the death penalty again was misinformed. However, the Home Secretary was empowered to commute the sentence on humanitarian grounds if he felt it appropriate. Lee's agonising experience brought about a wave of public sympathy and indignation typified by Queen Victoria who reacted strongly in favour of Lee, even though she had been personally acquainted with the murder victim. She made her feelings known in a telegram to the Home Secretary, 'I am horrified at the disgraceful scenes at Exeter at Lee's execution. Surely Lee cannot now be executed. It would be too cruel. Imprisonment for life seems the only alternative'.

The Home Secretary Sir William Harcourt.

Sir William Harcourt concurred and told a packed House of Commons, 'It would shock the feelings of everyone if a man had twice to pay the pangs of imminent death.'

The Home Office hushed up the results of an investigation that concluded that a simple mechanical fault had caused the failure of the scaffold, thereby allowing many people to believe that an innocent man had been saved from death by a 'miracle' – a view bolstered by news of his prophetic dream which he had related to two warders before being taken out to the scaffold. John Lee was now the celebrated 'Man They Could Not Hang'.

THREE

Patrick O'Donnell
The Man Who Avenged
the Phoenix Park Murderers

We were as men who through a fen
Of filthy darkness grope:
We did not dare to breathe a prayer,
Or give our anguish scope:
Something was dead in each of us,
And what was dead was Hope.

A little over a year after the trial of John Lee, his former fiancée Kate Farmer married former seaman James Parrish at St Marychurch, Torquay. The marriage took place in May 1886, but lasted barely five years before ending with a touch of scandal reported by the *Totnes Times & Gazette*, 2 May 1891:

> Interest in the Babbacombe murder of 1884 is, says a correspondent, being revived by the disappearance from St. Marychurch of a married woman named Parrish, the whilom sweetheart of John Lee, who was condemned to death for the murder, but whose sentence was commuted to one of imprisonment during her Majesty's pleasure, after several attempts had been made to carry out the capital sentence. A smack of romance is given to the case by the fact that simultaneously with the disappearance of Mrs Parrish, a painter named Pomeroy, of the same place was missed, and that neither has since returned. Not unnaturally, the names of the two are now generally associated, although there is little evidence to support the theory of an elopement. It is believed that the missing woman is at present located at Plymouth. Her husband was, strange to say, a witness in the case of the murder of James Carey, the informer in the Phoenix Park tragedy.

The murder victim referred to in the newspaper article, James Carey, was killed for betraying fellow conspirators of the self-styled Irish Invincibles, a nationalist group who had assassinated Lord Frederick Cavendish, the newly appointed British Chief Secretary of Ireland, and his

Kate Farmer, former fiancée of John Lee.

Lord Frederick Cavendish, son of the Duke of Devonshire.

Deputy, Thomas Burke, as they strolled unguarded to their residences in Phoenix Park, Dublin, on Saturday 6 May 1882. Four days earlier, the country had been plunged into crisis when Prime Minister William Gladstone made concessions to the Irish Land League party and released their leader Charles Parnell. He had been held in Kilmainham Gaol for six months for making 'violent speeches' against repressive government policies which caused severe hardship for tenant farmers summarily evicted from their homes by ruthless landowners. The deal, made in secret without consulting the Government's official representatives in Ireland, led to the indignant resignation of the Lord Lieutenant, Earl Cowper, and the Chief Secretary, William Forster. Replacements Earl Spencer and Lord Frederick Cavendish were hurriedly appointed and the two politicians were officially sworn in at Dublin Castle. Early that evening, a twenty-one-gun salute was fired in Phoenix Park to signify the completion of the ceremonial proceedings, and although he had only arrived in the city the night before, Lord Frederick Cavendish, second son of the seventh Duke of Devonshire, proceeded to walk alone to his lodge. His lordship knew the route well, for he had previously aided a previous occupant of the same post, his elder brother Lord Hartingdon. The Under-Secretary Thomas Burke left the castle a few minutes later in a cab, but seeing his superior walking through the park gate, alighted from the carriage and dismissed the driver. This blatant disregard of security, during a year that had already resulted in fourteen deaths and 1,500 incidents of civil unrest, was to prove fatal for the two colleagues as they fell in step and walked along arm-in-arm engaged in conversation, completely unaware that they were stepping into a carefully prepared ambush. Although a game of polo and a cricket match were in progress in the public park – also populated with cyclists, horse riders and pedestrians – the unwary politicians were suddenly set upon by two men wielding long double-edged knives. Witnesses looked on in horror as the defenceless men were slashed and mutilated by their assassins who then boarded a waiting hackney cab and made good their escape. The Lord Lieutenant, Earl Spencer, accompanied by his private secretary and a servant, had just arrived on horseback in the garden of the Viceregal Lodge when he heard a commotion which he took at first to be merely a common brawl. Little realising that leading Government ministers were being viciously assaulted, Spencer summoned a policeman to investigate the incident. The officer hurried to the scene of the heinous crime and discovered the bodies of the politicians lying in pools of blood on the roadside. Terrible wounds had been inflicted on the principal target of the assassination, Catholic Irishman Thomas Burke, denounced by nationalists as the leading 'castle rat' in the British 'occupation'. He was stabbed repeatedly in the back, neck and chest and pierced through the heart, before his windpipe was savagely severed. It emerged later that the Fenian terrorists did not even recognise the rich prize of Frederick Cavendish. Rushing forward to protect his friend, the Chief Secretary struck one of the assailants across the face with his umbrella and called him a 'ruffian' before running into the road where he was attacked and suffered a broken arm and cuts to his hands and face in trying to ward off blows, before the deadly blade was plunged into his side, neck and lungs. As he fell to the ground he was almost struck by two passing cyclists who hurriedly pedalled out of harm's way as they heard the dying man cry out, 'Ah! You villain'.

The shocking news was immediately relayed to William Gladstone, whose own niece was now the tragic widow of his protégé and former private secretary Frederick Cavendish. The Government offered a £10,000 reward for the apprehension of the perpetrators of this latest outrage to stain the nation's troubled history. The authorities had no clue as to the identity of the assailants until they themselves claimed responsibility for the politically motivated crime by delivering black-edged cards to newspaper offices bearing the words, 'Executed by order of the Irish Invincibles'. The hunt was now on to track down and bring to justice members of this hitherto unknown secret society.

The police investigation took a long time to suspect that the identity of the man instrumental in planning the vicious attack was one of the most prominent men in Dublin, James Carey. Everyone believed in the family man's piety and public spirit as he belonged to every religious and philanthropic organisation imaginable. He was also a successful businessman, owning a building company which had been awarded several large construction contracts. Another lucrative source of income was gained from sub-letting several tenement properties, which, it transpired, were also used for meetings by like-minded men of violence in a newly created brotherhood whose avowed intent was, 'To make history and to remove the principal tyrants of the country'. Carey was first arrested on suspicion in July 1882 then released without charge three months later. In the ensuing city elections, held in November, the hypocrite assumed the mantle of a wronged patriot to secure votes and convincingly won a seat on the council. The veneer of respectability was finally cracked when Carey was one of numerous members of his organisation rounded up and taken into custody in January 1883. Weapons including knives and guns had been discovered during a search of his home and while awaiting questioning, he was tricked into revealing his role in the conspiracy by police officers, who deliberately left a door open – allowing him to overhear their conversation giving Carey the impression that other suspects were ready to talk. The ruse worked and, believing that the police knew who else was involved, Carey pleaded for

Thomas Burke – primary target of the assassination in Phoenix Park.

The Irish Invincibles carry out the Phoenix Park Murders.

his life by confessing that he was the one who had 'suggested knives' for the operation. At the scene of the crime, he had pointed out Thomas Burke and his, then unknown, companion, to the band of cut-throats who on his order, given by waving a handkerchief, committed the double murder. When the case came before the magistrates in February, Carey was one of sixteen men who appeared accused of being involved in 'a conspiracy to assassinate government officials'. *The Times* commented that, 'A more wretched or repulsive group … could hardly be collected in Madame Tussaud's "Chamber of Horrors"'. Passions were running high amongst the prisoners as it was suddenly announced that James Carey was to appear for the prosecution and turn Queen's evidence against his former associates (including his brother Peter Carey), who hissed and jeered their former leader as he left the dock and climbed into the witness box.

Carey testified that he had been approached by London-based Fenians to form the Invincibles eighteen months earlier and took an oath, 'That of my own free will, and without any mental reservation whatever, would obey all orders given to me by the Irish Invincibles, nor to seek or ask more than was necessary to carry out such orders. The violation of which was death'. All the men in the dock, with the exception of one, were members of the organisation and money and weapons had been provided with the object of 'removing' prominent politicians, namely William Forster, Earl Cowper and Thomas Burke. Several attempts to eliminate the first two were foiled as their movements could not be accurately predicted. The day before Thomas Burke was murdered, the gang had assembled in Phoenix Park in the hope of apprehending their intended victim who failed to turn up when expected. They waited again the next day and were ready to accept failure yet again, when, shortly after 7 p.m., castle worker Joseph Smith, enlisted to identify Burke, called out 'Here he is'. Carey and Smith boarded a waiting cab driven by Michael Kavanagh and passed two constables as they travelled deeper into

The defendants deride James Carey as he prepares to give evidence for the prosecution.

Phoenix Park to where seven accomplices waited impatiently scattered in three groups. As planned, Carey waved his handkerchief to attract the attention of the waiting Joseph Brady, Timothy Kelly, Patrick Delaney, Thomas Caffrey, Michael Fagan, Daniel Curley and Joseph Hanlon. Curley was supervising the assassins and asked, 'Is he coming?' Carey replied, 'Yes, get the man in the grey suit'. As the politicians approached, Carey and Smith followed instructions from Brady to, 'Get the hell out of it'. Later that evening, Carey met up with Curley and asked, 'Is this true what I hear that Lord Frederick Cavendish and Mr Burke were murdered?' He affirmed, 'I believe it is'. Joseph Brady and Timothy Kelly carried out the attack which was described by Curley to Carey. 'Joe Brady knifed Thomas Burke in the back then knocked the other gentleman to the ground and killed him while Kelly slit the fallen Burke's throat'. Having fled from the scene, the assassins disposed of the murder weapons by breaking the blades into pieces and burning the handles.

Carey's evidence would subsequently condemn many of his associates to long prison sentences and five of the accused men, Brady, Kelly, Curley, Delaney and Caffrey, to death by hanging. The sentences were carried out separately during the month of May at Kilmainham Gaol. Executioner William Marwood travelled from England to Ireland disguised as a clergyman to avoid being recognised. A year earlier he had received a letter, postmarked Dublin, warning him never to set foot in the country on business again. The death threat was sent by the 'Secret Society of Assassinations'. When Marwood suddenly died three months after the execution of the Phoenix Park murderers, rumours abounded that he had been poisoned by his Irish enemies, prompting a belated inquest which ruled that he had died of natural causes after catching a chill on 'active duty'. A cynical Irish MP, commenting on Marwood's recent accomplishments while addressing a meeting, reminded the audience of the old saying that a man knew he lived in a civilised country when he saw a gallows. That being the case, his countrymen were safe in the knowledge that they currently enjoyed the 'protecting shadow of the gallows and the black flag'.

The act of self-preservation and betrayal against the nationalist cause meant that Carey's life was imperilled. He and his family could no longer remain in Dublin due to the threat of reprisals. Thus, he and his wife, with five children aged fifteen and under, changed their surname to Power and aided by the Government planned to start a new life in Natal, South Africa. Boarding a ferry to England, Carey's family were escorted by detectives to London, where they booked a passage on the *Kinfauns Castle*, bound for Cape Town. Meanwhile, Carey travelled separately and, undetected by his sworn enemies, survived the potentially dangerous journey across the Irish Sea, before holing up in Devon where he joined his family when the Royal Mail steamer made its scheduled call at Dartmouth. During the voyage to South Africa, 'Mr Power' foolishly dropped his guard and became friendly with passenger Patrick O'Donnell. Born in Donegal, O'Donnell had emigrated to Philadelphia and served in the Civil War before prospecting with little success in California, where he claimed to have worked as an agent organising lecture tours for such personalities as author Mark Twain. Although an American citizen, he remained committed to the Fenian cause, but was not known to have any association with any nationalist organisation. Having deserted his wife in America, he briefly returned to Ireland and acquired a mistress whom he passed off as a 'niece' known as Susan O'Donnell. Tired of eking out a living selling photographs of celebrated Irish-Americans, O'Donnell decided to try his luck in the gold mines of South Africa, complaining that 'America was played out'. He did not realise his travelling companion was a notorious informer until a steward showed him an illustrated newspaper article carrying a likeness of James Carey. Recognising the obvious similarity to James Power, O'Donnell's face turned white with anger as he fumed, 'If I had known he was on board the ship, I would have swung for him' and in a later conversation with a passenger vowed, 'I will shoot him and let daylight into the scoundrel before we reach the next port'. When the ship docked at Cape Town, O'Donnell changed his original plan to embark there and followed the Power family as they transferred to the *Montrose* for the final leg of their voyage to Natal. The following day, on Sunday 29 July 1883, when the vessel was off the coast of Port Elizabeth, O'Donnell invited Carey to join him for drinks in the second-class saloon bar, then produced a revolver from his pocket and shot the informer three times at point blank range. The dying Carey was comforted by his wife as his killer remained seated with his sobbing girlfriend clinging to him. When confronted by Mrs Carey, the gunman simply explained, 'I had to do it'.

The *United Ireland* commented that it would have been a more honourable option for James Carey to die in his homeland and be 'lying in the prison yard in a quick-limed shell' than to flee like a coward and be 'shot like a dog on a foreign shore'. Having escaped the gallows his death had been merely postponed for two months. The news was greeted with glee in Dublin. Bonfires were lit and

Executioner William Marwood.

an effigy of the informer set on fire and carried through the streets by a mob chanting and cheering the names of the Phoenix Park 'martyrs'. The Irish popular press observed that the Government's failure to protect a witness would inevitably dissuade anyone else from offering information in similar circumstances. The hatred felt for the informer was summed up in *The Freeman*:

> The cry which went up last evening in the thoroughfares of Dublin from the newsboys awakened only one query from the mouth of anyone 'Is it true?' Nobody was horrified, nobody pretended to be sorry, nobody was even surprised. The pervading feeling was, if the report were true, an event which the great bulk of people looked upon as a foregone conclusion had occurred with something approaching to precipitancy. … James Carey was as guilty of the awful murder of Lord Frederick Cavendish and Mr Burke in the Phoenix Park as was Joe Brady … Nobody that listened to his evidence came away than otherwise impressed that he was the most cold-blooded scoundrel that ever woman gave birth to. The callousness of his statement that he 'suggested knives'; the hypocrisy of his ruffianism in going to a meeting in the city and supporting a resolution deploring the murder in which he was principal; the infamy of his religious pretences; the audacity of his demeanour as informer, and approver, and murderer, all rolled into one, constitute character for the level of which one must descend to the lowermost stratum of human nature. There is no murderer or informer known to Ireland whose revolting memory is damned with a ban like that attaching itself to the name of James Carey.

The death of the ill-fated James Carey on the high seas was witnessed by Torquay-born James Parrish, who had been employed on board as the officers' servant for less than four months after leaving his previous occupation as the foreman of a soda water works in Cape Town. He was the first witness called for the prosecution at the murder trial held in London and testified:

> The day after we sailed I was leaving my berth to get tea ready for the officers at 3.45 p.m. As I entered the second-class saloon I saw Patrick and Susan O'Donnell drinking with another passenger

known to me as James Power. The O'Donnells were sitting on a settee with the woman's arm around the man's neck and resting on his shoulder, while Power stood facing them about a yard away. O'Donnell suddenly drew a pistol from his pocket and fired a shot at Power which struck him in the throat. As Power turned and staggered towards his wife's cabin, two more shots struck him in the back and he cried out 'Oh! Maggie, I'm shot'. Mrs. Carey came out of her cabin and caught the deceased as he was falling. I rushed past O'Donnell and saw him put the pistol into his left coat pocket. I found Power's wife lying at her husband's side, with her arms around his neck. I saw the blood spurting from Power's neck, and I placed my thumb on the wound and kept it there until the doctor arrived. I remained with Power until he expired about fifteen minutes later.

When cross-examined, James Parrish candidly admitted that he could have intervened and tackled the gunman after the first shot was fired but declined to do so on the grounds, 'I was afraid of being shot myself'.

Why O'Donnell chose to carry out the killing at sea instead of waiting to be put ashore where he could have done the deed secretly and planned an escape remains a mystery. Martyrdom by pleading guilty for the Fenian cause might have been the answer, but that proved not to be case when the defendant contradicted the account of James Parrish by trying to convince the jury that he had acted in 'self-defence'. According to O'Donnell, he was sitting alongside Carey having summoned him to the saloon to tell him, 'I want nothing more to do with you'.

To which the startled Carey replied, 'Why?'

O'Donnell then denounced his chum, 'You are James Carey the informer'.

James Parrish, eyewitness to the shooting of James Carey.

James Carey, his wife and eldest son who witnessed his death.

Realising his cover had been blown, Carey panicked and sprang to his feet producing a revolver from his pocket. Before he could use it, he was disarmed in a struggle with O'Donnell, who then drew his own weapon and fired at his adversary. However, it was noticeable that the young woman who had accompanied the gunman on the voyage and had witnessed the incident did not appear in court to collaborate the defendant's version of events. The police had provided Carey with a firearm for protection which was found concealed on the person of his eldest son Thomas, who upon witnessing the shooting brought it from the family's cabin with the intention of taking revenge on O'Donnell. If the defendant had snatched the gun from Carey, as he claimed, how had it got into the possession of the boy? As the prosecuting counsel summed up succinctly, 'If the testimony of Parrish is true, then the whole of the facts are before the jury'.

Having withdrawn to consider their verdict, the jury returned after some deliberation to seek guidance from the trial judge Mr Justice Denham. Despite hearing irrefutable evidence that the victim had received two of the three bullet wounds in the back while attempting to flee, they enquired whether a man using a weapon in the belief that another person was about to use one against him was guilty of manslaughter or murder. The learned judge quickly quashed this line of questioning by answering:

If you can honestly come to the conclusion, from the facts proved before you that Carey pointed the pistol and was about to take the life of the other man, then that other man, honestly believing that he was about to be shot, pulled out his revolver and shot him in order to prevent himself being shot; if you have this reasonable belief and think it is not a mere tale told to get him out of a difficulty, then I should say that would not be murder or manslaughter but honest self-defence. The question I put to you is this. Where is the evidence of anything amounting to an act by Carey that would induce the prisoner to think that?

Patrick O'Donnell on trial for the murder of James Carey.

The jury reconvened to their deliberations then tested Mr Justice Denham's patience once more by returning for an explanation of the term 'malice aforethought'. The judge reiterated the prisoner's difficulty in proclaiming innocence when, not content with one shot, he had continued to fire at a defenceless man. The medical evidence also showed that it was the third and final bullet which had proved fatal. There was no evidence of provocation, nor any evidence of a heated quarrel resulting in the pair wrestling with a firearm. Therefore, the jury could only assert the prisoner's innocence if they could escape the conclusion that the defendant had deliberately intended to carry out the shooting planned with 'malice aforethought'.

Having retired for a total of two hours the jury finally returned a verdict that the accused was guilty of murder. Donning the black cap, Judge Denham addressed the prisoner on the folly of taking the law into his own hands, no matter what his victim had done:

> The jury have come to the conclusion that you did fire the pistol, that you did kill James Carey, and you did it under such circumstances that you could not properly or honestly say that you did it in self-defence, or did it in such a way as to reduce your offence to manslaughter. I must say that I do not disagree with the verdict. … It would be a most lamentable thing in any civilised land to accept that the taking of a man's life – wicked though he might be – full of crime, hypocritical, abominable though he might be – was justifiable.

Upon hearing the death sentence pronounced, O'Donnell struggled with prison warders as they tried to lead him from the dock. Breaking free from his guards the prisoner shouted out defiantly, 'Three cheers for Ireland and the United States. To hell with the Britishers and the British crown. It is a plot against me'. The condemned man was hanged at Newgate Prison on Monday 17 December 1883. Executioner Bartholomew Binns, 'carried out his dreadful task with great efficiency', according to a correspondent who covered the grisly event for *The Times*:

Charles Parnell.

Arrived at the place of execution, O'Donnell was conducted to the scaffold and placed immediately under the beam from which the noose was hanging … Having received the necessary indication … Binns stepped forward, and touching a lever the unhappy man disappeared from sight. The body fell with tremendous force and velocity … The rope, which had made a cutting noise as it passed through the air, quivered for a second or two and then became perfectly still and motionless. … Immediately the execution took place a warder on the roof of the gaol hoisted the black flag and the bell of St. Sepulchre's ceased to sound the death-knell of the man who had thus paid the last penalty of the law and expiated upon the scaffold the crime of which he had been convicted.

The Phoenix Park atrocity dealt a mortal blow to the optimism created by the 'Kilmainham Treaty' – the informal understanding reached between intermediaries of William Gladstone and Charles Parnell. In the words of the outgoing Chief Secretary William Forster, 'The knives of the assassins cut asunder any ties between the National party and the Government'. Whilst riding in a carriage through Dublin, the new Lord Lieutenant, Earl Spencer, was stopped and berated about the plight of the country, when the horses' reins were grabbed by Anna Parnell, prominent political activist sister of Charles Parnell, the leader who had dedicated the Irish Land League to gaining for agrarian workers the three 'fs': free sale, fair rent, fixture of tenure, and the pursuance by peaceful means of 'Home Rule'. Charles Parnell's dream of finding a solution to his country's 'troubles' died with him in 1891. Shortly after her brother's death Anna Parnell moved to Ilfracombe. Living there under an assumed name, Cerisa Palmer, she kept in touch with Irish affairs and returned home briefly to campaign for the first Sinn Fein candidate to stand for parliament in a by-election held in 1907. Whilst residing in the north-Devon region she pursued her passion as a talented artist until her accidental death by drowning whilst bathing in the sea in September 1911. This revered pioneer of the women's movement lies buried in the cemetery of Holy Trinity church, Ilfracombe.

FOUR

OSCAR WILDE:
The Man Whose Love Dare
Not Speak its Name

This too I know – and wise it were
If each could know the same –
That every prison that men build
Is built with rocks of shame,
And bound with bars lest Christ should see
How men their brothers maim.

During the trial of the Phoenix Park murderers, informer James Carey revealed that plans had been laid by the Irish Invincibles to assassinate the Lord Lieutenant of Ireland, Earl Cowper. One of Carey's houses in Dublin was to be used as cover to shoot the earl as he left the seat of Government at Dublin Castle but the plot was abandoned when he resigned his position in 1882. Resuming his seat in the House of Lords, the politician made a statement following the fiasco at the attempted execution of John Lee and proposed that a full-time executioner should be appointed to replace part-time hangmen suggesting, 'it would be easier to get a good man for a permanent place, of say, £200 or £300 a year'. Earl Cowper may well have had inside information about the 'Babbacombe Murder' for he was the nephew of Lord and Lady Mount-Temple, neighbours of the victim Emma Keyse. They resided at the elegant villa Babbacombe Cliff, soon to become the centre of a sex scandal involving Oscar Wilde and his lover Lord Alfred Douglas, familiarly known as 'Bosie'.

The eminent Irish author was married to Constance, a favoured distant cousin of Lady Mount-Temple who was widowed in 1888. Four years later, while her ladyship was wintering on the Continent, she rented her villa to the Wilde family. The details were confirmed in a letter from Oscar in November 1892:

> Dear Lady Mount-Temple, I need hardly say how grateful Constance and I are to you for your
> kindness in promising to let us have your lovely house at Babbacombe, where Constance has passed

Earl Cowper was a target of the Irish Invincibles.

such beautiful days. I hope you will not mind my writing to you on business matters. If you would allow us to have it for three months for £100, we would both feel very grateful to you, and I need hardly say we will take the greatest care possible of your lovely home, and remember always who its chatelaine is, and how gracious is her courtesy in permitting us to sojourn for a season in her own house.

If you would let us carry out the scheme we propose we would have the great joy of being still more in your debt for many kindnesses and gracious acts. Believe me, truly yours, Oscar Wilde.

Babbacombe Cliff was a temple to the Pre-Raphaelite movement, its owner sharing the tastes of her artistic guest. The mansion's interior had been designed by John Ruskin, Oscar's former tutor on Florentine Art at Oxford University. Each of the bedrooms, named after a flower, such as marigold and daffodil, was decorated with themed wallpaper by William Morris, while magnificent artwork by Rossetti and Burne-Jones adorned the walls of the drawing room known as 'Wonderland'. Wilde, the leading apostle of the aesthetic movement felt perfectly at ease in this room and used it as a study to complete a new work *A Woman of No Importance*. He gave a summary of the play to the press, 'In the first act a letter, addressed in a woman's handwriting, is handed to the hero. He opens it, and reads it, and the men who are standing near ask him who is the correspondent. "Nobody in particular", he says, "it comes from a woman of no importance"'. To the impertinent suggestion that the theatre-going public might think it a play of no importance, Oscar delivered a typical repost, 'My dear fellow, as if anything I wrote could be of no importance!'

John Ruskin designed Babbacombe Cliff.

The arrival of the literary genius coincided with an important period in Torquay's history which celebrated its Charter of Incorporation in November 1892. As a result the town was granted more powers of self-government and the subsequent election of their first mayor, Councillor John Splatt. His wife was a leading light in amateur dramatics and was in the process of directing the first provincial production of Wilde's previous play *Lady Windermere's Fan* which had proved a huge success in London. The author generously supervised a rehearsal and attended a performance during its week-long run at the Torquay Theatre and Opera House in January 1893. He was wholesome in his praise of the production and presented magnificent bouquets of flowers to the leading ladies, although the audience were hugely disappointed when he declined to give a speech after the final curtain due to a sore throat – surely one of the few occasions in his life when he was lost for words. However, according to the *Torquay Times*, the master of the epigram was in fine form when an 'eminent artist' dared to question the public admiration for *Lady Windermere's Fan*, 'I much doubt whether such a work can outlive the present season. Now the School for Scandal has lasted for a hundred years, and is as popular today as ever it was'. 'Ah!' retorted Oscar, 'but so is Bradshaw's Guide [to railway timetables]'.

Accompanied by their two young sons, Cyril and Vyvyian, the Wildes enjoyed a family holiday, sailing and bathing on the nearby beach, the scene of the infamous 'Babbacombe Murder'. During his stay, Wilde was interviewed by Percival Almy who in 1959 would make a startling revelation to a local historian, while refusing to elaborate that John Lee's deliverance from the gallows had been arranged, 'Take it from me, the hangman was got at'. Early in 1893, Almy was a twenty-one-year-old newly qualified solicitor who had just obtained a position as

Charter of Incorporation ceremony, Torquay, 1892.

Percival Almy interviewed Oscar Wilde.

assistant town clerk in the newly formed Torquay Corporation. He would later set up his own successful legal practice and become the author of poetry and several guidebooks on Devon. In an article which was published in *The Theatre*, he recorded Wilde's thoughts on a wide variety of topics including literature, history, theology and notably, in view of the catastrophe that was to soon engulf him, his view on criminals, 'Never attempt to reform a man, men never repent'.

Early in February, Constance left her husband and children at Babbacombe Cliff while she sailed to join friends in Florence. Anticipating her departure, Oscar made overtures for another object of his affection to join him:

> My Own Boy, Your sonnet is quite lovely, and it is a marvel that those red rose-red lips of yours should have been made no less for music of song than for madness of kisses. Your slim gilt soul walks between passion and poetry. I know Hyacinthus, whom Apollo loved so madly, was you in Greek days.
>
> Why are you alone in London … come here whenever you like. It is a lovely place - it only lacks you … Always, with undying love, yours Oscar

'Bosie' was supposedly cramming for an examination at Oxford University with a private tutor who had just arrived at his mother's home in Salisbury. In correspondence with a friend, the tutor, Campbell Dodgson, explained how he had only worked with his pupil for a single morning before suddenly discovering that they were leaving for the coast:

Oscar Wilde.

He [Bosie] then quietly informed me at lunch that we were going to Torquay that afternoon to stay with Oscar Wilde! I gasped amazed, but I am phlegmatic and have a strong constitution, so I bore the shock well, and resignedly spent the whole afternoon re-packing the portmanteau I had just unpacked. Our departure was dramatic; Bosie was as usual in a whirl; he had no book, no money, no cigarettes and had omitted to send many telegrams of the first importance. Then with a minimum of minutes to catch our train, we were required to overload a small pony chaise with a vast amount of trunks while I was charged with a fox terrier and a scarlet morocco dispatch-box, a gorgeous and beautiful gift from Oscar. After hurried farewells to the ladies, we started on a wild career, Bosie driving. I expected only to drag my shattered limbs to the Salisbury infirmary, but we arrived whole at the station.

When we had been gone an hour or so, it occurred to Bosie that he had not even told Oscar we were coming, so a vast telegram was sent from Exeter. We finally arrived about nine o'clock and dined luxuriously. This is a lovely house, full of surprises and curious rooms, with suggestions of Rossetti at every turn. It is Lady Mount-Temple's and is lent to Oscar Wilde. Our life is lazy and luxurious; our moral principles are lax. … We … play with pigeons and children and drive by the sea.

Oscar sits in the most artistic of rooms called 'Wonderland,' and mediates on his next play. I think him perfectly delightful with the firmest conviction that his morals are detestable. He professes to have discovered that mine are just as bad. … I shall probably leave all that remains of my religion and my morals behind me.

With the arrival of his new guests, Wilde immediately contacted Lady Mount-Temple requesting an extension of his stay at Babbacombe Cliff:

Dear Lady Mount-Temple, As I suppose Constance has told you, I have returned to your lovely house in order to be with the children while she is away, and if you will still allow me I will gladly and gratefully accept your kind invitation to stay on for a couple of weeks more - till March 1st if it will not inconvenience you, as I find the peace and beauty here so good for troubled nerves, and so suggestive for new work.

Indeed, Babbacombe Cliff has become a kind of college or school, for Cyril [his eldest son] studies French in the nursery, and I write my new play in Wonderland, and in the drawing room Lord Alfred Douglas - one of Lady Queensbury's sons - studies Plato with his tutor for his degree at Oxford in June. He and his tutor are staying with me for a few days, so I am not lonely in the evenings.

Constance seems very happy in Florence. No doubt you hear from her. I venture to enclose the formal tribute due to the Lady of the Manor, and with many thanks for your kindness remain most sincerely yours Oscar Wilde.

The carefree holiday at Babbacombe ended in tears and tantrums when Bosie stormed off alone after a lover's tiff. The couple had an emotional reunion at the Savoy Hotel in London, before the student returned to Oxford and received a letter in similar vein to the one sent from Babbacombe:

Bosie, you must not make scenes with me. They kill me, they wreck the loveliness of life. I cannot see you, so Greek and gracious, distorted with passion. I cannot listen to your curved lips saying hideous things to me. … You are the divine thing I want, the thing of grace and beauty; but I don't know how to do it. … Why are you not here, my dear, my wonderful boy?

Wilde little realised that the terms of endearment expressed in these letters to Lord Alfred Douglas would later be produced as damning evidence against him in a court of law, for whilst at Oxford, Bosie gave an old suit of clothes to an unemployed clerk whom he had befriended named Alfred Wood. The down-and-out found a bundle of Wilde's letters in the pockets and extorted money from the author who felt compelled to hand over £35 in exchange for the correspondence on the pretext that he was enabling Wood to start a new life in America. However, Wood had passed on other letters to two professional blackmailers named Allen and Clibborn. They made copies of the letter written at Babbacombe Cliff beginning, 'My own boy, your sonnet is quite lovely' and signalled their intention by forwarding one to actor-manager Beerholm Tree, who was then rehearsing the play *A Woman of No Importance* at the Haymarket Theatre. Warned by Tree, Wilde was prepared when Allen turned up at his family home in London and played a dangerous bluff.

'I suppose you have come about my beautiful letter to Lord Alfred Douglas', greeted Wilde. 'If you had not been so foolish as to send a copy of it to Mr Beerholm Tree, I would gladly have paid you a very large sum of money for the letter, as I consider it to be a work of art'.

'A very curious construction can be put on that letter', insinuated Allen.

'Art is rarely intelligible to the criminal classes', rejoined Oscar.

Allen started negotiations, 'A man has offered me £60 for it'.

Seemingly unperturbed the author suggested, 'If you will take my advice you will go and find that man and sell him my letter for £60. I myself have never received so large a sum for any prose work of that length: but I am glad to find there is someone in England who considers a letter of mine worth £60'.

Allen was taken aback by his victim's calm demeanour and mumbled weakly, 'The man is out of town', then changed tactics and apologised for his actions which, he said had been brought about through his desperate need for money. A relieved Wilde handed him a half sovereign for 'expenses' and as he showed his unwelcome guest to the door, promised to send Allen a copy of the work when it was published in 'sonnet form'.

To Wilde's surprise, Clibborn, the third blackmailer, turned up five minutes later with instructions from Allen to return the original of the letter. When the bewildered victim asked, 'Why?' Clibborn expressed regret. 'Well, he says you were kind to him, and there is no use trying to rent you [slang for blackmail], as you only laugh at us'. Whereupon, Wilde gratefully handed over another half sovereign, thanked the criminal for his pains and saw him off with a light-hearted reproach, 'I am afraid you are leading a wonderfully wicked life'.

Wilde had succeeded in recovering the potentially damaging letter, in which he had complimented his young friend's 'rose-red lips' but unbeknown to him, a copy had found its way into the hands of a sworn enemy, Bosie's father – the Marquess of Queensbury.

Lord Alfred Douglas was estranged from his bullying parent, a situation that Wilde had earlier tried to alleviate while taking lunch at the Cafe Royal in London. Spotting the marquess in the dining room, he encouraged Bosie to pay his respects and invite his father to join them. The men had a convivial conversation and Queensbury accepted an open invitation to visit Babbacombe Cliff, although he subsequently failed to finalise the arrangement. It soon became clear that his son's continuing association with the author infuriated Queensbury who was determined to break up what he considered to be a, 'loathsome and disgusting relationship'. This involved a

Marquess of Queensbury, 'the most infamous brute in England'.

confrontation at Wilde's home, where, accompanied by a prize fighter, the author of the boxing rules which bear his name, demanded an interview and during a heated verbal exchange crowed, 'I hear you were thoroughly well blackmailed for a disgusting letter you wrote to my son'. Wilde defended the correspondence as a 'a beautiful letter' and asked, 'Do you seriously accuse your son and me of improper conduct?' Queensbury snarled, 'I do not say you are it, but you look it, and you pose as it, which is just as bad'. As the intruder was ordered out, Wilde told his servant, 'This is the Marquess of Queensbury, the most infamous brute in London. You are never to allow him to enter my house again'. The personal vendetta conducted by the aristocrat culminated in February 1895, when he left his calling card at the Albemarle club. On the back he scrawled an insult, 'For Oscar Wilde posing as a Somdomite [a misspelling of "sodomite"]'. This incitement was gleefully described by Queensbury as a 'booby-trap' and encouraged by Bosie; Wilde fell for the ploy and applied for a warrant for the noble's arrest on charges of criminal libel. Ignoring the advice of close friends, who did not consider that a jury would rule against a father concerned about the welfare of his son, he pressed ahead with the legal action, convincing his eminent prosecuting counsel Edward Clarke that there was no justification whatsoever in the allegation.

When the case came to court in April 1895, Oscar indulged in humorous banter with defence counsel Edward Carson. Asked whether he had adored any man younger than himself, he replied, 'I have never given adoration to anybody except myself'. Onlookers were enraptured by his wit as he parried cross-examination on the morals of his published works with withering sarcasm. However, private detectives had uncovered a catalogue of sordid liaisons enjoyed by the author with a number of rent boys. Realising the dangerous course that the questioning was suddenly taking, Clarke persuaded his client to withdraw his prosecution and the case was sensationally dismissed with enormous costs awarded to the defendant.

Based on the evidence obtained by Queensbury, Wilde was then arrested on charges of, 'committing gross indecency with other male persons' – a euphemism for any sex act between males which were then illegal. Knowing that the compromising letter from Babbacombe Cliff would be brought up by the prosecution, Edward Clarke addressed the matter first by questioning his client who cleverly passed it off as a 'prose poem'. Wilde was equally convincing when quizzed by the prosecution about the homosexual overtones of the poem *Two Loves*, written by Lord Alfred Douglas which ends:

> *'What is thy name?' He said, 'My name is Love'.*
> *Then straight the first did turn himself to me*
> *And cried, 'He lieth, for his name is Shame,*
> *But I am Love, and I was wont to be*
> *Alone in this fair garden, till he came*
> *Unasked by night; I am true Love, I fill*
> *The hearts of boy and girl with mutual flame'.*
> *Then sighing, said the other, 'Have thy will,*
> *I am the love that dare not speak its name'.*

When asked to explain the meaning of 'the love that dare not speak its name?', Wilde replied:

'The love that dares not speak its name' in this century is such a great affection of an elder for a younger man as there was between David and Jonathan, such as Plato made the very basis of his philosophy, and such as you find in the sonnets of Michelangelo and Shakespeare. It is that deep spiritual affection that is as pure as it is perfect. It dictates and pervades great works of art, like those

The concluding chapter in the trials of Oscar Wilde.

of Shakespeare and Michelangelo, and those two letters of mine, such as they are. It is in this century misunderstood, so much misunderstood that it may be described as 'the love that dares not speak its name', and on that account of it I am placed where I am now. It is beautiful, it is fine, it is the noblest form of affection. There is nothing unnatural about it. It is intellectual, and it repeatedly exists between an older and a younger man, when the older man has intellect, and the younger man has all the joy, hope and glamour of life before him. That it should be so, the world does not understand. The world mocks at it, and sometimes puts one in the pillory for it.

This eloquent answer drew admiring applause from the public gallery and the jury were clearly impressed by the defendant's confident display. This had to be weighed against the evidence of self-confessed male prostitutes and blackmailers such as Alfred Wood who had returned from America. Having deliberated for nearly four hours, the jury failed to reach a verdict, therefore the judge ordered a retrial. During the interim the press conducted a vindictive campaign against the author and when he returned to court, the defendant, who had been refused bail, was described as a 'broken man' by his counsel. Looking ill and dishevelled, Wilde was subdued in the witness box and there was none of the brilliant repartee that had marked his earlier appearances. The court heard about the author's 'ill-assorted friendships' with working-class young men whom he had treated to dinner, trips and lavish gifts, having been introduced to them during his frequent visits to a male brothel. Members of staff from the Savoy Hotel also testified to finding stained sheets on the bed which the author had shared with an unnamed youth. Faced with this overwhelming evidence, Wilde was found guilty and sentenced to two years' imprisonment with hard labour after the trial judge, Mr Justice Wills did him no favours in summing up the case for the jury:

> Whatever may be the guilt or innocence of the accused, it is clear that Mr Wilde has been obliged, from the result of the Queensbury trial, that his conduct, especially with regard to Lord Alfred Douglas, has been such that Lord Queensbury was justified in applying to him the words of the original libel.

Referring to the significance of the two letters written at Babbacombe Cliff and the Savoy Hotel, the judge asked:

> Is the language of those letters calculated to calm and keep down the passions which in a young man need no stimulus? It is strange that it should not occur to a gentleman capable of writing such letters that any young man to whom they were addressed must suffer in the estimation of everybody, if it were known. Lord Queensbury has drawn from those letters the conclusion that any father would draw, although he seems to have taken a course of action in his method of interfering which I think no gentleman should have taken, whatever motives he had, in leaving at the defendant's club a card containing a most offensive expression. This was a message which left the defendant no alternative but to prosecute or else be branded publicly as a man who could not deny a foul charge.

Conspicuous by his absence at the trial was Bosie who, at Wilde's insistence, had not been called to give evidence in his defence. Fearing that he might be arrested on similar charges, the young man travelled out of harm's way to Paris. Having reflected on the situation that had led to his conviction, Wilde wrote *De Profundis* – a bitter open letter attacking his young lover. It chronicled the author's spectacular fall from the pinnacle of literary success to abject public humiliation and degradation, giving a detailed account of his obsessive relationship with a demanding, petulant, self-centred young man and recognising the moment when he should have followed his instincts to end it:

> When at the end of March '93 you left my house at Torquay I had determined to never to speak to you again, or to allow you under any circumstances to be with me, so revolting had been the scene you had made the night before your departure. You wrote and telegraphed from Bristol to beg me to forgive you and meet you. … I consented to meet you, and of course I forgave you. On the way up to town you begged me to take you to the Savoy. That was indeed a fatal visit for me.

Before the hearing of the criminal libel case, Wilde completely ignored the affect the attendant publicity may have on his wife. Persuaded by one of Bosie's selfish whims, the pair went off to take a break in Monte Carlo, where Oscar covered the entire cost of travel, hotel accommodation and his lover's losses at baccarat. Meanwhile, Constance Wilde sought refuge with Lady Mount-Temple at Babbacombe Cliff. Whilst staying there she wrote a letter seeking guidance from a society fortune-teller Mrs Robinson, 'What is to become of my husband who has so betrayed me and deceived me and ruined the lives of my darling boys?' The lady had already given the answer two years earlier at a party at the Haymarket Theatre after the London opening of *A Woman of No Importance*. Basking in the glory of his latest success the author consented to have his palm read and was noticeably distressed when told that his right hand revealed that he

'My wallpaper and I are fighting a duel to the death'.

would, 'send himself into exile'. The prediction proved correct, for, following his release from Reading Gaol in 1897, Wilde fled to France where he would spend the last three years of what *The Times* described in his obituary as, 'a life of wretchedness and unavailing regret'. His spirit broken by his fall from grace, financially ruined by legal costs and grief-stricken and guilt-ridden by the premature death of his wife shortly after his release from prison, Wilde's health swiftly deteriorated and he wryly acknowledged that, 'I am dying beyond my means'. Residing in a seedy hotel, he gazed at the drab décor of his dismal room and commented, 'My wallpaper and I are fighting a duel to the death. One or other of us has got to go'. A month later he passed away. Loyal friends bore the cost of his funeral and one of them complained with unintended Wildean wit, 'Dying in Paris is really a very difficult and expensive luxury for a foreigner'.

FIVE

CHARLES DE VILLE WELLS: The Man Who Broke the Bank at Monte Carlo

A prison wall was round us both,
Two outcast men were we:
The world had thrust us from its heart,
And God from out His care:
And the iron gin that waits for Sin
Had caught us in his snare.

When John Lee unexpectedly escaped the death penalty, he gained a reprieve when the ultimate sentence of the law was commuted to life-imprisonment. After serving brief periods in solitary confinement at Pentonville and Wormwood Scrubs, he spent seven years at Portsmouth Prison, working mainly in the laundry, before being transferred to work in the famous stone quarries and cutting sheds of Portland Prison in 1892. Two years later, the press published examples of the country's 'prison poetry' scrawled on the walls of cells by inmates. Recording their feelings and misfortunes in this way may not have matched the literary merit of Oscar Wilde's epic *Ballad of Reading Goal*, but there was practical prose from one experienced convict:

Milbank is thick shins and graft at the pump;
Broadmoor for all lags as go off their chump;
Brixton for good toke and cocoa with fat;
Dartmoor for bad grub, but plenty of chat;
Portsmouth, a blooming bad place for hard work;
Chatham on Sunday gives four ounces of pork;
Portland is the worst of the lot to joke in;
For fetching a lagging there's no place like Woking.

Life at Portland Prison was certainly no 'joke'. Known as the 'Prison on the Cliffs', the penitentiary enjoyed a reputation among convicts for harsh discipline, second only to Dartmoor, as the most reviled prison in the country. For many years Lee was punishment orderly and witnessed at close hand the inhumane birching and beatings meted out to prisoners, 'I have seen some terrible objects of bleeding humanity brought back to the punishment cells. Their faces alone – I could only look at them – bore testimony to the awful agony they had suffered'. The exploits of 'The Man They Could Not Hang' gave him celebrity status amongst his fellow inmates, fame that was shared by only one other prisoner, fraudster and gambler Charles De Ville Wells, immortalised in the popular music hall song as *The Man Who Broke the Bank at Monte Carlo*. He was born at Broxbourne, Hertfordshire in 1841, the son of lawyer and minor poet Charles Jeremiah Wells, whose prose, according to one admirer, 'might more naturally be mistaken, even by an expert, for the work of the young Shakespeare'.

The Wells family relocated to France where Charles junior finalised his education in Marseilles before pursuing various business interests across Europe. Having disposed of a successful company in Paris he returned to England in 1885 with a capital of £8,000 which was soon exhausted while residing in Plymouth where he determined to become a successful inventor. He provisionally applied for almost 200 provisional patents paying a fee of £5 for each, of which only a handful were followed up with applications for a full patent at a cost of £750 a time. According to a spokesman for the Patent Office, Wells submitted applications for 'everything under the sun' that included: a new type of confectionary, olive-oil purifier, mustard preserver, umbrella, sunshade, envelope opener, actuating fog horn, torpedo, navigable balloon, combined safety lamp and fire grenade, and machines for cleaning ships' bottoms and ventilating railway tunnels. However, the only one of Wells' inventions to achieve any measure of success was an idea for a musical skipping rope which he sold for a paltry £50. Unperturbed he advanced to a far more ambitious project which was to bring about his downfall. Coming up with an idea to radically improve the efficiency of steam engines which, he claimed, would reduce the amount

Prisoner John Lee.

Wells was pointed out to Lee as they laboured in different work parties.

of coal fuel used by half, he took out advertisements in the press to attract investors to back his invention in return for a share of fabulous profits. Setting up a London office, where a clerk dealt with responses from 3,000 interested parties, Wells acquired the necessary capital to fit out six vessels at Plymouth. The pride of the fleet was the luxury yacht *Palais Royal*, which boasted a ballroom, music room and sumptuous accommodation for sixty guests, necessary, the investors were assured, as a showpiece to promote the new improved engine. In July 1891, the inventor 'tested' the vessel while sailing in the Mediterranean. Accompanied by a mistress thirty years his junior, beautiful artist's model Jean Paris, the yacht called at Monte Carlo. From this moment on, business was to become secondary to gambling when Wells enjoyed extraordinary luck at the roulette wheel. Boldly placing even money bets on red and black, he won on virtually every spin of the wheel until he finally exceeded the 100,000 francs 'bank' allocated to each table. On these extremely rare occasions, attendants ceremoniously covered the table with a black 'mourning' cloth and closed it for business for the rest of the day, signifying that the 'bank' was temporarily 'broke'. However, this was to be no fluke by Wells, who during a five-day spree broke the bank a total of twelve times. At one stage he won twenty-three times out of thirty spins of the wheel and sailed away with £40,000. These extraordinary feats of good fortune at the roulette wheel gained the winner celebrity status in the press and before long, music-hall star Charles Coburn was featuring a song written by Fred Gilbert and inspired by the gambler's success. As the tune's popularity spread, it was soon heard being sung in public houses and was played on every street corner barrel organ. Whenever Wells entered a nightclub or restaurant, the orchestra would strike up his signature tune *The Man Who Broke the Bank at Monte Carlo*.

The casino hired detectives to observe Wells at the tables, convinced that he was either cheating or beating the house with an unfathomable system. The gambler put his success down to the ability to ride a lucky streak, 'Anyone is free to watch me play and imitate me, but the general defect of the ordinary casino gambler is that he lacks courage'.

Wells triumphed at the tables again in November 1891. He placed his opening bet on number five, at odds of 35 to 1. Incredibly, his number came up. Leaving his original bet and his winnings on the table, five came up again. This happened five times in succession. Out came the black cloth and Wells raised another fortune of £20,000 when he broke the bank a further six times. However, his gambler's 'courage' was to be tested to the limit when he returned to Monte Carlo for a third time in October 1892. The winning 'system' – the principle of which he attributed to having discovered when developing his wondrous fuel-saving engine – finally failed him. His

The Casino at Monte Carlo, 1891.

Wells' vessels were anchored at Plymouth.

amazing run of luck came to a ruinous end as he began to lose, lose, lose. He gambled every penny he had – what remained of his previous winnings and the money invested in his company – before trying to win it back with further cash he persuaded his investors to part with, on the pretext that his yacht had caught fire and expensive 'repairs' had to be made to his fuel-saving engine. Doubling his stake to recoup his losses had disastrous results compounding his reversal of fortune.

By the time the *Palais Royal* sailed home and anchored in Plymouth Sound, proceedings to sue the yacht's owner had been instigated to recover monies owed to bilked investors. To avoid facing his creditors in court, Wells withdrew the last £5,000 of investors' money from his account, mortgaged five of his ships, the *Kettledrum, Kathalinde, Isabella, Ituria* and *Wyverne*, then fled from Plymouth on his last remaining vessel and landed at Le Havre, where he was reduced to selling the coal from the yacht's tender to raise more funds. Word of his impending arrival had been passed across the English Channel to the British Consulate and he was picked up by the gendarmes just as he was preparing to set sail again. It transpired that he had been wanted in France since 1883 for fraudulently selling shares in a tramway company. The local authorities only agreed to the extradition of Wells on condition that the *Palais Royal* remained behind and was put up for sale to repay his swindled Gallic creditors.

The man who broke the bank at Monte Carlo was brought back to 'face the music' in London at the Old Bailey and stood trial on charges of fraud in March 1893. Onlookers revelled at the embarrassment suffered by the biggest losers in Wells' steam-engine scam – two young members of prominent families, Catherine Mary Phillimore, a notable author and daughter of a deceased High Court Judge, Sir Robert Phillimore and the Hon. William Henry Crosby Trench, heir to the title of his brother Lord Ashtown – who had foolishly parted with figures approaching £20,000 and £10,000 respectively. All of the people duped by Wells had sent a £5 fee, supposedly to allow Wells to submit an application for the patent, and many others, including the Reverend Aldrich-Blake, parted with a further £750 so that the inventor could obtain a full patent for his vaunted fuel-saving steam engine. No one checked to discover that Wells had never patented the device at all – furthermore, it was discovered that the *Palais Royal* was propelled by nothing more than its original engine described by the ship's former captain as 'antiquated'. Gullible investors were also informed that negotiations were ongoing with foreign governments interested in the innovation and were soothingly assured, 'Now all is right, and our harvest is here'. However, instead of the expected cash 'profits', further worthless share certificates were issued. Trench and Phillimore both testified that they had come under pressure from Wells to continue forwarding money as their reputations were threatened with ruination by the defendant. Using tactics akin to blackmail, they were informed by telegram that unless more funds were forthcoming, their involvement in the failing French company would be exposed. Wells & Co. was unlimited, thereby the shareholders were all individually and personally liable for the mounting debts. Referring to the company funds lost at roulette, Wells hinted darkly at criminal consequences for, unless 'a quiet liquidation of the whole business' could be obtained, 'they would all be in trouble'. The prosecution told the jury that the defendant was not a member of the Institute of Civil Engineers as he frequently claimed in his correspondence.

In desperation, the defence called a mechanical engineer, Hermann Eschen, who told the court that he had carried out a variety of work in connection with the defendant's patents. During the period from 1887 until 1892, he had made 'all sorts of models' from plans supplied. Among them was a device for using less steam which took 'a great deal of time and labour' to prepare from Wells's technical drawings. Several engines were constructed for saving consumption of coal on board and fitted to vessels at Plymouth. Some credibility was given to Wells's mechanical knowledge when portions of a cylinder were produced in court and Mr Eschen pointed out the salient features of the invention which would affect a saving of fuel – 'assuming it would work'. To a facetious question asked in cross-examination, the witness confirmed that he had not been involved in constructing many of the defendant's other innovative contraptions such as the 'musical skipping rope'. In summary, the witness confirmed that he had always received payment for his work from Wells whom he regarded as carrying on 'a bona fide business' and being 'a hard-working man'.

Unfortunately, having heard all the evidence, the jury did not agree with Herman Eschen's assessment of the prisoner. Upon delivering their verdict, trial judge Mr Justice Hawkins, clearly irritated by the 'inordinately long' amount of the time the case had taken, criticised the prosecution's insistence on presenting a 'hundredweight of documents' to support the twenty-three indictments, before summarily handing out a stiff sentence to Wells. The outcome of the trial was the subject of a leader in *The Times* that was more scathing in its criticism of the hapless victims than the convicted conman who was afforded a measure of grudging admiration:

The picturesque career of MR. CHARLES WELLS - commonly described upon placards as 'Wells of Monte Carlo' as if he were some sort of Italian watering-place - has been terminated or grievously interrupted by a sentence of penal servitude for eight years. His counsel laboured to represent him to the jury as an honest and hard-working inventor who, after fifty years of commercial rectitude, had been thrown off his balance by winning £40,000 in five days at the gaming tables. Englishmen have so much sympathy with gambling, combined with so much love of austere moralizing about its evils, that this pretty theory was not at all ill-contrived to divert attention from the previous misdeeds of

The Man that Broke the Bank at Monte Carlo.

I've just got here, through Paris, from the sunny
  southern shore,
  I to Monte Carlo went, just to raise my winter's
  rent;
Dame Fortune smil'd upon me as she'd never done
  before,
  And I've now such lots of money, I'm a gent,
  Yes, now I've such lots of money, I'm a gent.

Chorus.

  As I walk along the Bois Boolong,
  With an independent air,
  You can hear the girls declare—
  He must be a millionaire.
  You can hear them sigh
  And wish to die,
  You can see them wink the other eye
  At the man who broke the bank at Monte Carlo.

I stay in doors till after lunch, and then my daily
  walk,
  To the great Triumphal Arch is one grand triumphal
  march,
Observed by each observer with the keenness of a
  hawk,
  I'm a mass of money, linen, silk, and starch.
  I'm a mass of money, linen, silk, and starch.

I patronised the tables at the Monte Carlo hell,
  Till they hadn't got a sou for a Christian or a Jew;
I then flew off to Paris for the charms of mad'moiselle,
  Who's the loadstone of my heart—what can I do
  When with twenty tongues she swears that she'll
  be true?

————————

The popular song inspired by the good fortune of Charles Wells.

MR. WELLS. The jury, however, declined to regard the prisoner in the interesting light of a victim to a not unamiable weakness, and the jury undoubtedly did well. In another sense it is true that the breaking of the bank at Monte Carlo was the beginning of the end for MR. WELLS. It lifted him into notoriety – a thing which every judicious swindler ought to avoid. … To the student of life and character it is disappointing that we know all to little history of MR. WELLS. … He is fifty-one, and the exploits which have attracted such an inconvenient amount of attention are all matters of the last two or three years. … How and when did he make the fascinating discovery that the world is well stocked with people who have money but no brains? … There is a splendid simplicity about MR. WELLS'S methods which may have been reached by intuition, but is more probably the outcome of long experience. We can imagine him as a juvenile rogue concocting really elaborate and ingenious methods for affecting the redistribution of wealth. … Whatever he may have been in his fervid and exuberant youth, it is only in the age of potboilers that we know him. He simply advertised himself as the possessor of a valuable patent languishing under the cold neglect of a careless world, but ready to bestow wealth beyond the dreams of avarice upon any one who would trust him with moderate sums. For a paltry advance of £475 he offered MR. TRENCH no less than £6,000. For a further £500 he offered another share worth £6,000 in the lucrative business he was promoting. Then he offered £50,000 for a further advance of £1,250, and subsequently for £2,000 more, he offered a total of £150,000. By this delightfully simple method he extracted over £9,000 from that extremely disingenuous young man. From MISS PHILLIMORE he obtained no less than £18,000 by identical representations. To the REV. F. ALDRICH-BLAKE he offered £100,000 as a first charge upon the profits of his patents in return for £1,500, which sum duly paid in two instalments. Nothing could possibly have been easier or simpler. These excellent people knew nothing at all about MR. WELLS or his patents, or his company, or the subjects with which the patents were supposed be concerned. No trouble or apparatus was necessary to effect their deception. An absolute stranger merely presented himself with a cock and bull story backed by gorgeous promises, and they poured their money into his lap. The vulgar confidence trick of the pothouse loafer is not more absolutely elementary.

It is really open to question whether it be not a misnomer to call this sort of thing fraud. To satisfy any reasonable conception of fraud there ought surely to be some illusion or deception which, though perhaps obvious to an expert, is ingenious enough to excuse the blunder of persons using only ordinary common sense. But in this case there is nothing of the kind. WELLS had no deep-laid scheme and no misleading stage properties. He simply said to these people in effect – give me a thousand pounds today, and at some future day I will give you fifty thousand. It really is an arguable question whether expensive legal machinery ought to be maintained to protect people who voluntarily give away their money to the first stranger who says he would like it, adding some preposterous promise which ought not to take in a child of ten. Nor does it seem unfair to point out that a knave like WELLS trades entirely upon the unreasonable cupidity of his dupes. How can any man of probity suppose that he is in any way entitled to such exorbitant remuneration as WELLS offered? How can he suppose that if £100,000 were really paid him for the loan of £1,500, the money could possibly have been honestly earned? Even if the transaction were, in a sense, genuine, is it not very plain that it is a gamble just as truly as staking money at Monte Carlo, and therefore, a thing which men of high principle ought to be under no temptation to touch?

The mystery of Charles Wells' past history, posed in *The Times* leader, was partly answered when he gave evidence at his subsequent bankruptcy hearing. Wells amused onlookers by telling the court that as he was accompanied by two prison warders he could hardly dispute the fact that he had been convicted of obtaining money by false pretences and fraud. Married in 1866, Wells had subsequently abandoned his wife and children and admitted to the court that he had not provided maintenance for his family nor entered into a legal marital settlement. Following the breakdown of the marriage he had pursued a number of business interests across Europe – refining sugar in Russia, mining in Spain, manufacturing paper in Paris –– before relocating to Plymouth, then London. Referring to the international fame and notoriety gained by his success at the casino in Monte Carlo, Wells explaining that he had not 'speculated' at the tables but had 'solved the problem' of how to win by studying roulette playing over a period of six years until he came up with a method which, until recent catastrophic events, he believed to be infallible. Using stake money put up by an American, whom he declined to name, he had accrued a grand total of £60,000 in winnings, of which his share was £20,000. Some of the money had been spent on the costly upkeep of the *Palais Royal*, while the casino had since more than recouped their losses. He did not consider that what he had done was 'gambling' because he sat at the tables from noon until midnight which he considered to be, 'absolute hard work'. His failure at the casino coincided with the failure of his business and at the time of his arrest, the only registered participants in his Paris-based company Wells & Co. were himself, the Hon. Crosby Trench and Miss Phillimore, who had both expected to receive vast sums promised to them in excess of £250,000. To gales of laughter, Wells confirmed that the figures had been arrived at to the satisfaction of his two out-of-pocket partners. For the past five years he had been engaged in financing patents. He could not submit a list of how many patents were currently held in his name, 'unless the warders would be kind enough to accompany me to the Patent Office'. All his papers and accounts had been burned during the unfortunate fire on his yacht, the *Palais Royal*, which had been bought for £3,500 in 1891 and had subsequently cost a further £22,000 to refurbish the vessel in extravagant style in order to entertain grandees viewing models of his steam-engine invention in continental ports. A proposed sale of the yacht for £20,000, to a Baron De Bret, fell through when the French authorities seized the vessel at Le Havre. As to the remainder of his fleet, the *Kettledrum*, acquired in 1890 for £400, had recently been mortgaged

Convicts at work in the quarries of Portland Bill.

for £300 to pay a solicitor's bill. In August 1891, he purchased the *Kathlenda* for £1,500 which he had also mortgaged for £765 to pay for work carried out on the vessel. The *Isabella*, *Ituna* and *Wyverne* obtained in 1888 had recently been signed over in lieu of money owed to the Hon. Cosby Tench – although he neglected to tell the gentleman that the latter vessel had been 'shipwrecked'. He did not recognise Trench and Phillimore as creditors as they had been major shareholders in a now defunct limited company, but accepted other liabilities of some £8,000 with unrealised assets worth an estimated £13,000. Unsurprisingly, the defendant's figures were disputed by the Official Receiver who contended that there was a far greater sum unaccounted for by the debtor.

The bankrupt swindler served the customary period of solitary confinement at the outset of his prison sentence and was then transferred to Portland Prison, where he was pointed out to celebrated inmate John Lee as they laboured in different work parties. A strict ban on talking among inmates was enforced in the penitentiary and the only activity affording any social contact was provided by the daily divine services in the prison chapel, where 'Babbacombe' Lee was a member of the choir – accompanied on the organ played by 'Monte Carlo' Wells.

Granted remission and released in March 1899, Wells changed his name to Charles Davenport and with Jeanette Paris posing as 'Mrs Davenport', settled in Cork where he subsequently hatched another scheme which landed him back court in November 1905. He was charged with obtaining £6,000 from investors in a bogus company, the South & South-West Coasts Steam Trawling Fishing Syndicate, which, in actuality, owned two steam launches and only one trawler which was not even seaworthy. In the dock with Wells was his accomplice, the Reverend Vyvian Henry Moyle who, whilst serving as the Vicar of Eston, Middlesbrough in 1873, had been the subject of scandal when jailed for eight years for selling forged share certificates in a scam that fraudulently realised £30,000. Despite being a convicted felon, the cleric somehow convinced the Bishop of Reading that he was fully repentant and was reappointed to the living of Ashampstead – a position he held for several years until he experienced 'financial difficulties', neglected his parish duties and was removed from his post. To the disbelief and disgust of the trial judge, Moyle claimed that none of his past misdemeanours had led to him being unfrocked. To attract investors to their non-existent fishing fleet, Moyle & Wells, alias Davenport, advertised extensively in the national newspapers. Interested parties received convincing letters of recommendation from the Reverend Moyle, 'You cannot do better than invest what you can afford in this excellent business … Three old valued friends of mine have become investors for substantial sums … all practical and hard-headed men of business, and not likely to mix themselves up with any shams'. In answer to an enquirer, who thought the proposed high level of profits to be 'incredulous', Moyle explained that the syndicate could obtain higher prices for catches landed at Cork, 'We have six steamers at work and have struck a rich fishing part in Ireland which has not been fished before'.

Committed for trial on charges of 'conspiracy to defraud and obtaining money by false pretences and obtaining credit while an undercharged bankrupt' Wells complained that he was unable to persuade anyone to put up a £1,000 bail surety as, 'writs were flying like bats'. When the trial commenced in February 1906, the two defendants, both undischarged bankrupts, changed their plea to 'guilty' in the face of irrefutable evidence that no fishing had ever been carried out on behalf of the syndicate. In his defence, Wells was described by his lawyer as a man with an, 'ingenious and clever turn of mind and poetic imagination'. The Recorder agreed that Wells had certainly devised an 'ingenious fraud', in which Moyle had been a 'plausible tool for taking people in' and sentenced the accused to three years and eighteen months imprisonment respectively.

Wells' signature tune could be heard on every street-corner barrel organ.

Paroled after serving only half of his sentence, Wells entered into matrimony with his long-time companion Jeanette Paris. The marriage ceremony was also a sham as the groom chose to be married in the name of James Burns at Fulham Registry Office in 1908. The pair would also form a criminal partnership, culminating in the robbery of their own bank!

In July 1910, Wells adopted the name Lucien Rivier and opened a bogus bank in Paris offering to pay 1 per cent a day interest to investors, equivalent to a too-good-to-be-true annual return of 365 per cent. Over a period of eight months, 60,000 people were taken in by the scam, investing a total of £120,000, attracted by a circular which boasted, 'There may exist firms which guarantee no loss in Stock Exchange transactions; ours is the only one which assures a constant daily profit'. Predictably, the shady bank suddenly closed for business and the couple took off with their ill-gotten gains in a newly acquired luxury yacht named *Harbinger* and anchored off the coast of Falmouth. The money swindled from investors was placed in bank accounts opened in the names of Charles and Janet De Ville, before the long arm of international law caught up with the fugitives, who were detained by a police officer from Scotland Yard in January 1912.

Following a protracted and unsuccessful appeal against extradition proceedings, seventy-year-old Wells was forced to return to France and face justice for his latest crime spree. The trial resulted in a further period of imprisonment for five years on charges of fraudulent bankruptcy and obtaining money by false pretences.

Charles De Ville Wells alias Charles Davenport alias James Burns alias Charles De Ville alias Lucien Rivier was buried in a pauper's grave when he passed away in 1926. Celebrated in life as the 'man who broke the bank at Monte Carlo', the incorrigible fraudster met his maker as the man who died broke and bankrupt in Paris.

SIX

HERBERT ROWSE ARMSTRONG: The Man Who Planned the Perfect Murder

The loftiest place is that seat of grace
For which all worldlings try:
But who would stand in hempen band
Upon a scaffold high,
And through a murderer's collar take
His last look at the sky?

John Lee fully expected to be released after serving twenty years' imprisonment which was the usual period served by reprieved murderers. He was not informed that as a bungle on the scaffold had brought about his survival, not the merits of his case, the Home Secretary of the day, Sir William Harcourt, had recommended that the prisoner should remain in confinement for the remainder of his natural life. Press rumours of Lee's imminent release in early 1905 led to unwarranted intervention by the Archdeacon of Westminster, Basil Wilberforce, Chaplain to the House of Commons, who opposed parole for the prisoner on the grounds that he had threatened to 'do for' all those who had given evidence against him. Furthermore, he informed the Home Office that he 'knew the Lee family well' and that they were 'a well-known witch family on Dartmoor'. According to the deluded churchman, there was a legend in Devon that 'no Lee could ever be hanged' as John Lee's mother had also escaped the death penalty (a distorted myth attributable to the case of her cousin Mary Jane Harris and 'baby farmer' Charlotte Winsor - see Chapter 2).

Basil Wilberforce was the grandson of slavery abolitionist William Wilberforce, and a close personal friend of the late Lord and Lady Mount-Temple. His comments to the Home Office were based on nothing more than local superstition and gossip gathered during his previous visits to Babbacombe Cliff, where he supported her ladyship's work for the temperance cause at meetings of the Blue Mission. This unreliable source of knowledge did not prevent the Home Secretary, Aretas Ackers-Douglas, from using the false allegations to turn down a suggestion that

John Lee in middle age.

he should exercise clemency for Lee. Answering a question tabled by a member of the House of Commons, the Secretary of State repeated Wilberforce's claim that he could not consider such a course of action as, 'the convict had constantly repeated threats against the lives of many now living'. When denied his freedom, Lee was bitterly disappointed and decided to launch an orchestrated campaign for his release. A letter to his mother was published in the *Manchester Sunday Chronicle* urging readers to raise petitions and contact their local MPs to lobby the Home Secretary and persuade him to reverse his decision. The prisoner's mother Mary Lee also engaged the services of Newton Abbot solicitor Herbert Rowse Armstrong to help her in the fight for justice for her son. Acting on her behalf, Armstrong wrote to enlist the support of Harry Eve, the member for the prisoner's home constituency, who merely passed on the request to Ackers-Douglas with an apologetic rider which made his own unsympathetic position perfectly clear:

Dear Mr Home Secretary, I am sorry to trouble you but in my constituency lives the mother & some other relatives of the convict John Lee who was sentenced some 20 years or so ago for the murder of Miss Keyse at Babbacombe. I believe three attempts were made to carry out the sentence at Exeter Gaol but without success.

Would you please read the enclosed communication which has reached me from the solicitor who has been writing for the mother & tell me if anything can be done in the matter. I feel it is too bad to bother you but I am in rather an awkward position as Miss Keyse was an acquaintance of me & my family & if I do nothing it will perhaps be said that I am influenced by prejudice against the convict. So I venture to trouble you & will apologise for so doing. I remain Yours faithfully, Harry T. Eve

Canon Wilberforce.

Mary Lee campaigned for her son's release.

Harry Eve MP.

Reluctantly forwarded for the attention of Aretas Ackers-Douglas was the offending correspondence from Herbert Rowse Armstrong to Harry Eve:

Dear Mr Eve, I had hoped to have the pleasure of seeing you on Friday, and, as I learn that it may be some little time before you are in Newton, I am taking the liberty of writing you on a matter.

Twenty years ago John Lee was convicted at Exeter of the murder of a lady at Babbacombe, and was sentenced to be hanged. Three attempts were made to carry out the sentence without success owing to the executioner's bungling and the death sentence was commuted to penal servitude for life.

I have been acting professionally for his mother and have had some correspondence with the Home Office as to the prospect of his sentence.

The only result has been that 'the Secretary of State regrets that he cannot advise interference with the sentence …' once the convict has served 20 years and subsequently 'that he will not be released when he has served 20 years.'

I am quite aware that there is no statutory definition or power to diminish a life sentence, but the Home Office regulations do constantly allow of its reduction to 20 years and often less e.g. Mrs. Maybrick – as to almost nullify the effect.

In the present case the convict has reached the highest class for good behaviour and the evidence on his conviction in the first instance was purely circumstantial.

Unfortunately, the local papers have been causing a considerable fuss with wild conjectures unauthorised and undesired by Mrs. Lee, which possibly are reflected by official action.

Under these circumstances and in view of recent proceedings of the Home Office, would it be possible for you as Member of this Division to put a question in the House, or even raise the matter on the Home Office ... .

At present, I understand the convicts position anomalous: as there are no regulations by which a man, who has served more than 20 years, can obtain further good conduct marks, or reach a higher class - inferentially presuming release at such a period of continuous good conduct has taken place. I must apologise for the length of this letter but I feel so strongly that the matter is one which shouts to be taken up.

I am yours faithfully, H. Rowse Armstrong

The writer of this letter little realised that a quarter of a century hence, he, like the aforementioned Florence Maybrick, would deny charges of poisoning a spouse and be condemned to stand on the scaffold. The difference was that there would be no reprieve for Armstrong who would go down in the annals of criminal history as the only solicitor ever to be hanged for murder.

Born in 1869 at Plymouth, Herbert Rowse Armstrong gained a degree at Cambridge University where his small stature contributed towards his selection as deputy coxswain for the annual Oxford-Cambridge boat race. He completed his legal training as an articled clerk in Liverpool, then in 1901 joined the firm of Hutchins & Hutchins who had branches in Teignmouth, Torquay and Newton Abbot, before setting up in business on his own, in the latter market town. Here, his professional manner, gentlemanly bearing, immaculate attire and pleasant personality impressed people and made him a very popular figure in the district. Living with his mother and two maiden aunts they all attended the local Congregational church where Armstrong was made a deacon and appointed secretary. As a lieutenant in the Devon Volunteers, he was the driving force of the Newton Abbot section of the Torquay Company of Royal Engineers and proved successful in increasing its strength and efficiency. It was a proud moment for the dapper officer when he led his men to serve as a guard of honour to King Edward VII at

Ernest Hutchins employed Armstrong at Newton Abbot.

King Edward VII lays the foundation stone at Britannia Royal Naval College, 1902.

Dartmouth where His Majesty laid the foundation stone of the Britannia Royal Naval College in 1902. Four years later, Armstrong accepted a business opportunity in the Welsh border town of Hay-on-Wye and established himself in practice with solicitor Edmund Hall Cheese before returning to south Devon where he married his fiancée of three years, Katherine Friend, at the parish church of her home town, Teignmouth, in June 1907. After a honeymoon in Switzerland, the couple settled down in Wales and within three years Armstrong was made a full partner in the firm of Cheese & Armstrong, then acquired a fine home, Mayfield, employing a housekeeper and maidservant to help his wife cope with their family of three children. In the spring of 1914, his financial and personal standing in the community grew when he became the sole owner of the law firm following the sudden and unexpected deaths of Mr and Mrs Cheese who succumbed within a day of each other.

Up to this point, the Armstrongs appeared to have a reasonably content marriage, but the seven-year itch in 1914 and the advent of the First World War was to change matters. Armstrong had continued his military interest as a member of the Territorial Army and during wartime was called upon to serve in various locations on home soil, attaining the rank of major which he retained upon his return to civilian life. It is clear that during this period of military service he dallied with other women and met a widow to whom he would subsequently propose marriage, once the imposing obstacle to this union had been removed – his nagging wife Katherine. She 'who must be obeyed' had a shrewish disposition and imposed strict rules on her household. It was widely known among their friends and acquaintances that she 'henpecked' her husband. He was only allowed to smoke in one room of the house and discouraged from imbibing alcohol, except on rare occasions for medicinal purposes; she was once heard to say in company, 'I think you may have one glass of port Herbert; it will do your cold good'. People felt sorry for the little man who was routinely humiliated in his own home. 'Six o'clock, Herbert, how can you expect punctuality in the servants if the master is late for his meals.' Famously, she turned up at his tennis club and summoned him home in the middle of a match by reminding him loudly in front of other members that it was his 'bath night'.

Demobbed in 1919, Armstrong found it hard to pick up his neglected business and soon ran into financial difficulties. As his law practice floundered in 1920, he was apparently more concerned about a patch of dandelions on his lawn and, despite employing the services of a jobbing gardener, bought several quantities of arsenic to treat them himself. By August 1920, Katherine Armstrong was in failing health and her eccentricities increased to the point that the family physician, Dr Hincks, worried about her mental health, had her placed in a private asylum at Gloucester. Certified insane, suffering from delusions and visions, she improved substantially and was allowed home after six months' treatment in January 1921. Thereupon her condition deteriorated rapidly and the following month she passed away. Her bereaved husband made a curt note of the event in his diary 'K died'. On the day his good lady was buried at Cusop Dingle churchyard, the four people who attended detected the cheery mood of the chief mourner as he chatted about fishing rights as the coffin was carried from the home to the hearse. Major Armstrong was now free to enjoy a full social life where smoking and drinking were no longer banned. He held dinner parties at Mayfield but had difficulty in getting fellow solicitor Mr Martin, with whom he was professionally involved on opposite sides of a protracted property sale, to accept an invitation to his home. Armstrong persisted with a flurry of offers for his rival to attend dinner or tea and finally persuaded him be sociable. Martin came to tea and ate a buttered scone which was placed on a plate by his apologetic host with the words, 'Excuse fingers'. Later that night, Martin was violently ill and two months later on New Year's Eve 1921, the locality was shocked to learn that the major had been arrested for attempted murder. Sensation and gossip flared as the police investigation then switched to the churchyard where the body of Katherine Armstrong was exhumed and medical examination found evidence to suggest that she had been poisoned.

Having meticulously planned and patiently carried out the perfect murder of his wife, Armstrong's reckless pursuit of Oswald Martin led to his appearance in the dock of the court at Hereford. Indicted for murder and attempted murder, the trial jury heard that the prisoner had been under suspicion for some time. Some months previously, Martin had anonymously received a box of chocolates in the post, which were subsequently found to have been injected with arsenic after a dinner guest fell violently ill minutes after consuming one. Armstrong used the same method to treat dandelions, filling a syringe with individual preparations which he wrapped in packets. A packet of arsenic was found on his person soon after his arrest which he attempted to conceal from the police. When the trial judge asked the accused why he did not deal with the dandelions by simply pouring on the weed killer, he answered vaguely, 'I really don't know. At the time it seemed the most convenient way of doing it'.

Katherine and Herbert Rowse Armstrong.

Motives for his wife's murder were soon made evident: money and another woman. The victim's sister, Ida Bessie Friend, travelled from her home in Torquay, and testified that Katherine had made a will in 1917 which had been witnessed by herself and another Torquay lady, Augusta Gertrude Hutchins, who was then acting as nurse-companion to the deceased. The £2,500 estate was divided into a small bequest for her long-serving housekeeper, with the remainder to be put in trust for the three children, while her husband was not left anything. It emerged that when Katherine had been released from the asylum she had immediately changed her will naming her spouse as sole beneficiary. Armstrong had then evidently forged his wife's signature on the new instructions which were in his handwriting. The two household servants had signed as witnesses, although the women did not know what they were signing, nor had they seen their mistress make her signature on the document, rendering it invalid. Addressing the subject of the major's love life, the court was stunned to learn from a physician that, while the major's wife was confined at the lunatic asylum, he had consorted with prostitutes and contracted a sexually transmitted disease. Furthermore, within three months of his wife's death he had proposed marriage to a fifty-year-old widow, Marion Gale, whom he had met during wartime. Appearing as 'Madame X' to conceal her identity, the heavily veiled object of the poisoner's affections told a hushed courtroom that she had first met the major in 1915 when he was serving as adjutant with the Royal Engineers at a camp near Christchurch in Dorset, and was billeted at a friend's house near her home in Boscombe. He had often visited her at her mother's home and talked about his wife and family. There was nothing improper in their relationship, but they had continued to keep in contact by letter when he was posted elsewhere. They met up once for dinner in

London, shortly before his wife was admitted for treatment, and she did not see him again before he was widowed, when he travelled down to her home in Bournemouth. Armstrong tentatively raised the question of marriage in May 1921, and formally proposed in August. She admitted having since visited his home but had felt unable to enter into marriage because of her responsibility to her infirm mother and a niece who was her ward, therefore they had agreed to reconsider the situation in twelve months' time.

Although 'Madame X' played down talk of marriage in court, three love letters found on Armstrong written by Marion during the Christmas period shortly before he was arrested, clearly demonstrate that life with him, cared for by servants, was a potential escape from her life of domestic drudgery, 'I am really between the devil and the deep sea and my mother is just at her most aggravating … and I am just sick of the whole show'.

Referring to the events that had brought them closer together she wrote, 'It is strange to feel that Xmas has come round again, and this year has brought great changes hasn't it, for both of us – I wonder how next year will find us'. Marion realised that prospects for the New Year were not good when she learned from the newspapers that her would-be fiancée was in custody. Her last letter, sent two days before the major's arrest, had a prophetic ring. On 22 December, Irene Wilkins was lured to her death in Bournemouth by Thomas Allaway, who was subsequently executed. Marion commented on the crime, 'Of course we all talk Murder – it is so absolutely baffling and apparently without motive'.

The 'Hay Poisoner' was apprehended when Oscar Martin was taken seriously ill in October after eating the buttered scone handed to him by Armstrong. Dr Hincks was called to treat the ailing solicitor and sent off a sample of his urine to a clinic for analysis. The result showed that it contained a substantial amount of arsenic. The truth suddenly began to dawn as chemist John Davies, who was Martin's father-in-law, revealed he had supplied Armstrong with quantities of the deadly chemical. Dr Hinks also realised that his patient Katherine Armstrong had suffered from similar symptoms. Their suspicions were referred for investigation by the police who finally acted when Martin became terrified by another barrage of invitations to dine with Armstrong. The major had been stalling on a property deal, in which he had a considerable financial stake, for over eighteen months, and the purchasers represented by Martin withdrew their offer. Even with his wife's inheritance, Armstrong was unable to refund a £500 deposit demanded by Martin's clients and was sliding towards insolvency, though how he believed the elimination of his business rival would improve matters is hard to fathom.

The trial judge, Mr Justice Darling, had given the defendant a hard time by following up questions put by the prosecution. Despite this, Armstrong had given a good impression and odds were being offered by bookmakers in favour of acquittal. The jury went out to discuss the case and their rather offhand approach for deciding whether a man should live or die was revealed by the foreman Tom Hopkins to the *Evening News*. When the twelve good men and true retired, 'We first of all we had tea', said Hopkins, 'then we went to another table, where twelve chairs had been placed for us and I tore a sheet of paper into twelve pieces for a ballot. Each man was asked to write either "guilty" or "not guilty" on his paper, fold it and hand it to the foreman'. When Hopkins announced the result there were eleven votes for 'guilty' and one for 'not proven'; the odd man out identified himself and said, 'Well Tom, you can guess whose the "not proven" is. I really believe the man is guilty'. Apparently this man bore a grudge against Mr Justice Darling and was trying to be obstructive. As he was obviously of the same mind as his colleagues, there was never any real doubt about the verdict. Hopkins said, 'We have heard enough of the case and need not discuss it any more. Let's have a quiet smoke before we go back to court'.

Major Armstrong's old friends in Newton Abbot greeted the outcome of the trial with incredulity; likewise, many people in Hay-on-Wye agreed that the mild-mannered major was incapable of such acts and upon his emergence from the first court appearance, a large crowd greeted him with 'three cheers'. If, having committed such a crime, it seemed extraordinary to his supporters that the accused would not eliminate all prospect of any suspicion arising against him in the future, by simply arranging for the body of his wife to be cremated. Defence counsel contended that Katherine Armstrong's mental state caused her to commit suicide but this notion was dismissed by the trial judge who reminded the jury of the victim's final words to her nurse, 'I'm not going to die am I? I have so much to live for; my husband and my children'.

An appeal on behalf of the defendant failed and Fleet Street editors agreed wholeheartedly with the verdict and suspected that other people had fallen victim to the 'Dandelion Poisoner'. Three weeks before Armstrong had made the attempt on Oswald Martin's life, a Hereford estate agent, Willi James Davies, died in a nursing home, having fallen ill with acute abdominal pains the day after having a business lunch with the solicitor where he had unsuccessfully tried to obtain money owed to a client. The simultaneous deaths of Armstrong's former partner Edmund Hall Cheese and his wife had also rather fortuitously made the major heir to the whole legal practice. These suspicions were laid bare in a hard hitting condemnation of the murderer which appeared in the *Daily Chronicle*, 1 June 1922:

There were two Armstrong - Armstrong the poisoner and Armstrong the social figure, the public man.

Armstrong the poisoner was as cold-blooded a criminal as ever went to the scaffold. The other Armstrong was a good-natured, affable little fellow, with many pleasing qualities.

Such was the many-sided personality of this abnormal character. Good and evil were so closely interwoven in his character as to present an amazing study in contradictions.

In his legitimate pursuits Armstrong showed himself to be a man of some ability. He was a capable lawyer and a clever after-dinner speaker.

As a poisoner he was a reckless bungler.

His attempts on the life of Mr. Martin were almost ridiculous enough for comic opera. A man of law, one might have expected, would have taken every precaution to cheat the gallows, but Armstrong, seemingly never even took the hangman's rope into consideration.

He tried time and time again to poison Martin with arsenic obtained from his intended victim's own father-in-law. Once he actually succeeded in administering poison, and Martin was attended by Dr. Hinks, the very doctor who must have observed that the violent symptoms were the same as shown by Mrs. Armstrong during her last mysterious illness. Yet, Armstrong was bent on taking Martin's life.

Surely he ought to have known, after 20 of his invitations to tea had been avoided by excuse and subterfuge, that he was suspected – that he was living in the shadow of the gallows.

But this never seems to have entered his mind. So little did he fear detection that he actually carried his stock-in-trade about in his pocket. Always he had with him that little packet of arsenic; there, in his pocket, he carried damning evidence of his guilt!

Perhaps it was that he had been lulled into a false sense of security. Mrs. Armstrong may not have been his first victim.

Palmer and Pritchard and other prisoners began their poisoning careers warily, but, as victim after victim was disposed of without suspicion aroused they threw caution to the winds, and were eventually brought to justice through their own carelessness.

Was Armstrong another such case?

The Armstrong case at the appeal court.

There is a cemetery in Hay, and another in Hereford, where will lie buried for all time what may be evidence of other crimes.

In these cemeteries rest the bodies of three persons, which, if exhumed, might yield up the same secret as that revealed when Mrs. Armstrong's body was taken from the quiet graveyard at Cusop.

Each of these three persons was well known to Armstrong; each died suddenly after a painful illness.

Two of them, a man and his wife, both advanced in years, were taken ill at the same time, and died within 15 hours of each other.

It was said that the third person had been Armstrong's guest at a tea-party for two at Mayfield, and that he was seized with an attack of vomiting in the train on the way back from Hay.

At the time there was not the faintest breath of suspicion. The deaths were certified as due to natural causes, and it was not until after Armstrong's arrest that people began to recollect the circumstances in a new light.

As no analyses were made in these cases, there will always be the doubt as to whether Armstrong was in any way responsible.

While the press speculated about the possibility that Armstrong was a serial killer, prolific thriller writer Edgar Wallace, who covered executions for the *Daily Mail*, had offered the then considerable sum of £5,000 to the condemned man to acknowledge his guilt, but although that money could have helped to secure the future for his three soon-to-be orphaned children, Armstrong refused the opportunity to make an exclusive 'confession' and was hanged at Gloucester Prison in May 1922, insisting to the end, 'I am innocent of the crime for which I have been condemned to die'.

SEVEN

ROBERT HICHENS:
The Man Who Sank the *Titanic*

Some love too little, some too long,
Some sell, and others buy;
Some do the deed with many tears,
And some without a sigh:
For each man kills the thing he loves,
Yet each man does not die.

At eight o'clock on the morning of the 18th of December, 1907, the iron gates of a prison opened, and out into the light of day stepped two middle-aged men.

One man was an official in civilian clothes. He bore the hall marks of drill and discipline. The other man …

The other man! He looked hunted and cowed like a creature crushed and broken. He seemed to hang back as if he were afraid of the light of day. He appeared to draw no happy inspiration from God's sunshine. He fumbled at his overcoat pockets as if the very possession of a pocket was a new sensation. He trod gingerly, as if the earth concealed a pitfall.

Away they went by cab and rail to Newton Abbot. There the two men walked to the police-station, where the official announced that he was a warder from Portland Convict Prison in charge of John Lee, convict, on ticket-of-leave.

John Lee handed his ticket to the police officer, who read it.

What was it that made the policeman start as he read? What was it that made him look so curiously at the tall, thin, clean-shaven elderly man before him?

It was this: Certain particulars on the ticket showed that on February 4th, 1885, the bearer was sentenced to death at Exeter Assizes for murder at Babbacombe. The man was 'Babbacombe' Lee.

'Babbacombe' Lee was on his way to spend Christmas with his aged mother – John Lee, the man they could not hang, the man under whose feet the grim mechanism of the scaffold had mysteriously failed in its appointed work.

The story of his life's ordeal John Lee himself will tell … It is the story of one, who, rightly or wrongly, was doomed in the first flush of manhood to a torture more fiendish than the human mind, unaided by the Demon of Circumstances, could have devised. It is the story of a man dangled in the jaws of death, and hurried thence to a living tomb whose terrors make even death seem merciful.

From his terrible ordeal, John Lee emerges with the cry, 'I am innocent' still on his lips. And who that has not suffered will not listen?

John Lee's long awaited return home, described above in the introduction to his rapidly published autobiography, was realised after spending twenty-three years in custody. His story published in a book and serialised in *Lloyd's Weekly News* attracted the interest of many women who offered marriage and in a letter to a male well-wisher he confided, 'I have dozens of sweethearts'. However, any hopes of a romantic reunion with his former fiancée Katie Farmer were crushed when she gave this interview to the press:

He has suffered. I hope his future life will be happy. His way will not be my way, for I am now settled in life after my vicissitudes. I hope he may be able to prove his innocence … I was then a silly sentimental girl, and did not know my own mind. I am wiser now … I remember most vividly the last time I saw him. It was at the inquest. I recall he walked with his head in the air, although he was in such deadly peril. He recognised me and smiled, and said, 'Goodbye, my dear'. Those words were the last words I heard him utter. He never sent a letter from prison to me, and never asked me to visit him in Portland. … My friends told me that Lee would be kept in prison as long as he lived, and a life's devotion would be thrown away. So I put him out of my heart.

After five years of marriage Kate had left her husband James Parrish, eye witness to the murder of Irish informer James Carey (see Chapter 3) and eloped to Plymouth with painter and decorator Frederick Pomeroy. Coincidentally, in the same issue of the *Torquay Times* which announced Lee's freedom, her former husband's name also appeared reporting his evidence at an inquest into the accidental death of his father Joseph Parrish. The elderly gardener had been tragically knocked down and killed by a runaway horse and carriage as he was walking home from a rugby match with fellow supporters of Torquay Athletic.

In January 1909, a little over a year after his release, John Lee married workhouse attendant Jessie Bulled in Newton Abbot at the Congregational church where his solicitor Herbert Rowse Armstrong had once been deacon until moving from the area following his own marriage to the woman he would subsequently poison (see Chapter 6). Immediately after the wedding ceremony, Lee and his bride took the train to Newcastle, where he had been offered employment making personal appearances for a brewery in a chain of public houses. The couple were blessed with the birth of a son in January 1910, before moving later that year to London where Lee obtained a similar position at Ye Olde Kings Head, Southwark. Within six months, he had run off with barmaid Adelina Gibbs, callously abandoning his wife who was expecting their second child. A daughter, who would never know her father, was born in August 1911. On St Valentine's Day 1912, Jessie was compelled to seek parish relief from the Lambeth Guardians. A report in the *Daily Mail* recorded her plight stating that her errant husband had, 'received a good salary for exhibiting himself, but in February last year he left for America and, after sending her help for some weeks wrote stating that he was out of work and could send no more money'.

John Lee and his lady friend had sailed from Southampton on the liner *Kronprinz Frederick Wilhelm* joining the thousands of immigrants crossing the Atlantic for a new life in the 'Land of the Free'. Two months after Jessie Bulled made her humiliating claim for financial assistance,

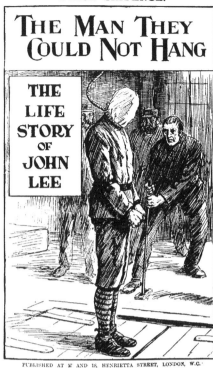

PRICE SIXPENCE.

THE MAN THEY COULD NOT HANG

THE LIFE STORY OF JOHN LEE

PUBLISHED AT 16 AND 18, HENRIETTA STREET, LONDON, W.C.

John Lee's autobiography published in 1908.

the world mourned the loss of 1,500 lives in maritime history's darkest hour – the sinking on her maiden voyage of the much vaunted SS *Titanic*. One of those who perished was the widely respected former editor of the *Pall Mall Gazette*, William Stead, who sat in the first-class smoking room calmly reading a book while the ship sank. A committed believer in spiritualism, clairvoyance and mental telepathy, he was the journalist who had related the role of his close friend Robert James Lees to a Chicago newspaper about the alleged unmasking of Sir William Gull as Jack the Ripper (see Chapter 1). Strangely, Stead had apparently foretold the *Titanic* disaster and had a premonition of his own fate. In his book *How I Know the Dead Return*, one paragraph begins, 'Let us consider the Atlantic as the grave'. The author then compares one shore with Earth and the other with the Eternal shore. In March 1886, he published an article entitled 'How the Mail Steamer Went Down in Mid-Atlantic, by a Survivor'. In the story an unnamed steamer collides with another ship and due to a shortage of lifeboats there is a huge loss of life. Stead comments, 'This is exactly what might take place and will take place if liners are sent to sea short of boats'. Uncannily, the event which sent him to a watery grave was graphically prophesised twenty years before his death in an article published in the December 1892 issue of the *Review of Reviews* – an international monthly magazine founded by himself.

In a tale entitled 'From the Old World to the New', Stead describes how a White Star liner, the *Majestic*, is carrying a group of English tourists across the Atlantic to visit the World Fair in Chicago when, one of the passengers, a clairvoyant, picks up a telepathic message from a friend who is close to death and floating helplessly in the water having survived the wreck of the *Montrose*, sunk after colliding with a giant iceberg that can be seen from the *Majestic*. The

Lee eloped to New York on the *Kronprinz Frederick Wilhelm*.

clairvoyant persuades the captain to put him out on a boat and his powers guide him to rescue the survivor. The setting of the story and the descriptions of the iceberg and the wrecked ship tally almost exactly with the fate of the *Titanic* – although by 1912, Marconi's wireless telegraph, not telepathy, sent an SOS to summon the rescue boat *Carpathia*.

Fact superseded fiction when White Star's *Titanic* emulated the fate of the fictional *Montrose*. At the helm of the ship at the moment of impact with the deadly iceberg was seaman Robert Hichens. He was then put in charge of a lifeboat and having been fortunate to escape with his life recounted the full horror of the catastrophe in an interview published in the *New York Herald*, 24 April 1912:

> From Robert Hichens, quartermaster at the wheel of the Titanic when the great vessel crashed into the iceberg, and then in command of one of the boats which left the steamship before it went down have come details of the terrible night at sea which could have been known to perhaps no other person. And standing out in memory of this young Cornishman are shrieks and groans that went up from the dark hulk of the giant steamship before she sank.
>
> Hichens, a type of young Englishman who follows the sea, had for years been on the troopship Dongolo, running to Bombay, and thought himself fortunate when he obtained his berth as quartermaster of the Titanic, the greatest and largest of all steamships. He told a HERALD reporter in their sequence the events of the night and morning of April 14 and 15.
>
> It was in his boat that Mrs John Jacob Astor took her place, after Colonel Astor had kissed her goodbye, and handed her a flask of brandy, then taking his place in the line of men, some of whom realized even then that the steamship was doomed. And his last sight as his boat was lowered was of Captain Smith, standing on the bridge, giving his orders as calmly as if he were directing her entrance into a harbour.
>
> He told of how the officers stood with revolvers drawn, to enforce, if the emergency should arise, that rule of the sea of women first, but how the emergency did not arise, and the men stood back or helped the women to their seats. In the way of a seaman he told the story of the night spent in the little boat, comforting as best he could the women who did not realise as he did that some of them had looked upon their loved ones for the last time.

William Stead calmly read a book while the ship sank.

"My watch was from eight to twelve o'clock." said Hichens last night. "From eight to ten o'clock I was the stand-by man, and from ten to twelve I had the wheel. When I was at the stand-by it was very dark, and while it was not foggy there was a haze. I cannot say about the weather conditions after ten, for I went into the wheelhouse, which is enclosed … The next order was from the second officer for the deck engineer to turn the steam on in the wheelhouse as it was getting much colder. Then the second officer, Mr. Lightoller, told me to telephone the lookout in the crow's nest.

" 'Tell them," he said, 'to keep a sharp and strict lookout for small ice until daylight and to pass the word along to the other lookout men.'

"I took the wheel at ten o'clock, and Mr. Murdock, the first officer, took the watch. It was twenty minutes to twelve and I was steering when there were the three gongs from the lookout, which indicated that some object was ahead. Almost instantly, it could not have been more than four or five seconds, when the lookout man called down on the telephone:- 'Iceberg ahead!' Hardly had the words come to me when there was a crash.

"I ain't likely to forget, sir, how the crash came. There was a light grating on the port bow, the a heavy crash on the starboard side. I could hear the engines stop, and the lever closing the water tight emergency doors … The Titanic listed, perhaps five degrees, to the starboard, and then began to settle in the water.

At the subsequent inquiry held in a New York hotel owned by Plymouth MP Waldorf Astor, husband of flamboyant socialite Nancy Astor, Hichens was accused, by another occupant of his lifeboat, of ignoring pleas to search the water for survivors. Canadian militia officer Major Arthur Peuchen, a yachtsman of many years experience, had been placed in the lifeboat in order to help the quartermaster and Fred Fleet, the lookout who had first spotted the iceberg, take the women and children to safety. Peuchen was immediately at odds with Hichens for the way he gruffly confiscated alcohol and insisted that the women take the oars while he held the tiller. When a whistle sounded from the *Titanic*, Hichens explained it was a signal from an officer to recall the lifeboats and pick up more passengers but, although their vessel was only carrying thirty people – half of its capacity – he refused the occupants' request to try and save their despairing loved ones. 'No, we are not going

'Officers stood with revolvers drawn, to enforce … women first'.

back to the boat', he said curtly, 'It is our lives now, not theirs'. As the ship disappeared beneath the waves, the cries and screams of people fighting for their lives in the water was plainly heard in the still night air. Once again the quartermaster turned down pleas to help possible survivors by cruelly summing up the situation, 'It's no use; there's only a lot of stiffs out there'.

Women were not called to the New York hearing, but made their feelings known about the surly Hichens to the press. The fabulously wealthy Margaret Brown, who would be later immortalised in the 1964 Hollywood film starring Debbie Reynolds as *The Unsinkable Molly Brown*, told how the callous seaman had been of little help or comfort as he sat in the back of the lifeboat bemoaning their fate and swigging whiskey, therefore, she usurped his authority and took command of the situation:

> We stood him patiently, and then after he had told us we had no chance, told us many times, and after he had explained that we had no food, no water and no compass I told him to be still or he would go overboard. Then he was quiet. I rowed because I would have frozen to death. I made them all row. It saved their lives.

Also in the lifeboat was eighteen-year-old Madeline Astor. She was in the early stages of pregnancy having spent a long honeymoon in Europe with her multi-millionaire husband Colonel John Jacob Astor, a relative of Waldorf and Nancy Astor. One of the richest men in the world, Astor's wealth could not assure his safe deliverance that fateful night and his body was found floating in the cruel sea with $2,500 in cash on his person. He went to his death bravely and was last seen on deck giving a salute as the ship plunged beneath the waves. A source close to his young widow confirmed that she and the other women had been placed in a lifeboat with a 'drunken sailor' and continued, 'His condition was such that he could not row the boat and therefore the women had to do the best they could in rowing about in the icy seas'.

Captain Smith bravely went down with his ship.

The belligerent, inhumane attitude and over-reliance on drink displayed by Hichens at this great moment of crisis was to resurface some twenty years later in Torquay, where he failed disastrously to make a living running pleasure-boat trips. It was in the same town, during the summer of 1906, that he had met his future wife, Florence Mortimore. She was visiting relatives in the resort, while he was on shore leave with the crew of a private yacht. The couple only spent a few hours together before Robert returned to sea the next day. However, he quickly made his feelings known in a letter to Florence:

> Dearest, I now take the opportunity of writing these few lines according to my promise hoping you are none the worse for your nice little walk last night. I only wish I had met you at five or six o'clock and I would have seen more of you. I suppose you don't know how I have taken rather a fancy to you. Robert Hichens, Yacht Ariano, Torquay

Following a whirlwind courtship, the couple were married within a few months at the parish church in the bride's home village of Manaton. Settling firstly in Torquay, where their first two of six children were born, then Southampton, where Hichens served as a quartermaster aboard mail boats and liners of the Union Castle and British India shipping lines before securing a prestigious appointment on the newly launched luxury liner *Titanic*. The maiden voyage on the largest ship afloat and the subsequent heartrending return home to his wife, who anxiously awaited news while expecting the couple's third child, would be the seaman's first and last crossing of the North Atlantic. Following the terrible maritime disaster, Hichens returned to sea, serving with the naval reserve during the First World War, after which he spent some time working with one of his brothers in South Africa. By 1930, he had relocated his family to Torquay and found employment as a tout, selling tickets to holidaymakers for pleasure-boat rides, before accepting the opportunity to own his own vessel, the *Queen Mary*. He purchased

John Jacob Astor was 'last seen on deck giving a salute'.

the motor launch from businessman Harry Henley for the sum of £160 of which he paid a down payment of £100 with the remainder to be paid within two years. The venture quickly failed and he was unable to repay the balance. Furthermore, Hichens had borrowed the deposit from a Mr Squires who seized the boat to settle the debt following a poor season's trading in 1931. Tourists had seemingly failed to be attracted to a trip around the bay on a vessel navigated by the man who sank the *Titanic*.

The loss of his business caused Hichens to turn to drink and by the end of that year, his wife had left him and moved back to Southampton. For the next two years her troubled husband scoured the country unable to find work and unreasonably chose to lay the blame for his predicament on the man who had sold him the boat. On his travels he acquired a revolver for £5 and journeyed to Torquay determined to kill Harry Henley upon his arrival on 12 November 1933. He looked up an old friend of twenty years standing, fisherman Thomas Holden and told him, 'There will be two less in Torquay tonight. I've come down to do Henley and myself'. By early evening Hichens was drinking with another acquaintance, docker Joe Stroud, who hearing of the plan and shown the revolver warned, 'Put it away. Don't be a fool. He isn't worth swinging for'. Worse the wear for drink the gunman appeared to see sense and replied, 'I'll take your tip, I shan't give the hangman a job'. Later, while walking near the harbour with Stroud, he saw Henley as the pair passed each other without exchanging a word. However, after closing time, having consumed rum in at least three public houses during the course of the evening, Hichens took a taxi, driven by Harry Scrivings, who dropped him off outside Harry Henley's house at Stentiford's Hill, Torquay.

Hearing a knock at the door, Henley came outside to see Hichens standing with both hands in his trouser pockets. 'Do you remember me Harry?', slurred the inebriated Hichens. 'Why of course I do' replied Henley, 'What do you want?' The unexpected caller asked him for money, saying 'I am on the ground I want you to pick me up'. Henley naturally replied 'Why do you expect me to pick you up when you owe me £60 already?' Hichens became apologetic 'I am sorry, it is all through the drink that I am like this'. Referring to the debt, the out-of-pocket Henley, who had made no attempt to recover the money owed to him, commented, 'I have to suffer for that as well as you. I won't lend you a penny because you have been a rogue and a scamp to me'. Hichens gripped the revolver in his right-hand pocket and demanded, 'Is that your last word?' To which his creditor replied, 'I wouldn't give you a penny piece if you were lying in the gutter'. Hichens then pulled out the pistol and with the words 'Take that', raised the weapon to the level of his target's head. In the dimly lit porch, Henley thought that Hichens was going to strike him with his fist and instinctively put up his arm to ward off a blow. Two gunshot explosions followed as Hichens fired the revolver at point-blank range and very nearly succeeded in his desire to kill his former business associate. One shot passed through the side of the victim's head above the right ear and came out cleanly through the same side of the head without causing any internal damage. Henley felt a searing pain and subsequently lost a lot of blood but was fortunate not to suffer serious injury. The second shot went downwards and wide as Henley pushed Hichens away and punched his assailant in the face giving him a bloody nose. Hichens fell to the floor giving Henley the opportunity to run away and summon the police. Meanwhile, the gunman got up and staggered 30 yards before laying down on the footpath, where he tentatively put the revolver to his head and pulled the trigger but the bullet passed harmlessly by. Taken to the police station in an intoxicated state, Hichens enquired, 'Is he dead? I hope he is. He is a dirty rat, I would do it again if I had a chance, I intended to kill him and myself, too. He has taken my living away'.

When arrested he had two letters on his person. One was intended for one of his siblings and read:

My dear little brother – Just a last note to you. You may come to identify my body as your brother. My home is gone – no dole – no pension – can't get an officer's berth – result death by my own hand. Dear brother convey my kind feelings to all the family. I am no coward but this robber has to go out also. He stole my launch and my living. You can read this the last. Your loving brother Bob.

The second letter was addressed to the editor of the *Sunday Chronicle*:

There will be some more to add to my book story - the last man at the wheel of the 'Titanic' – the world's greatest sea disaster. I am quite sane but tonight I shall shoot myself. It is time I got my man at Torquay, who stole my launch Queen Mary.

Hichens also asked that any money forthcoming for his story should be forwarded to his estranged spouse – 'the best wife in the world'.

The following morning at the Torquay Magistrates Court, Hichens was remanded in custody for a week, then committed for trial. Amazingly, following nothing more than first-aid treatment at Torquay Hospital, Harry Henley was fit enough to attend the hearing with his injured skull swathed in bandages. On 29 November 1933, the prisoner appeared at the Winchester Assizes with dressings on his wrists as he had made a desperate attempt to slash his wrists while held in custody.

Brought to trial for attempted murder, the prisoner received an extraordinarily sympathetic hearing. Despite the murderous attack having been fermenting in his mind for many months, the defence counsel contended that the incident had been precipitated only because his client was under the influence of alcohol. With an unintended pun he explained that since Hichens had

Robert Hichens giving evidence at the *Titanic* Inquiry.

gone through the terrible ordeal on the *Titanic* he had been 'sinking lower and lower' through drink. The defendant's previous good character and the fact that he appeared to be a 'broken man' influenced the lenient outcome of the case reported in *The Times*, 30 November 1933:

> Robert Hichens, 51, a ship's navigating officer, who was stated to have been at the wheel of the Titanic when she was sunk in 1912 after striking an iceberg, appeared in the dock at Winchester Assizes yesterday, charged with the attempted murder of Frederick George Henry Henley at Torquay on November 12 by shooting him. Hichens was found guilty and sentenced to five years' penal servitude. Mr. Justice du Parcq said it was a lighter sentence than he intended to give, but he had taken his past career into account.

Luckily for Hichens, the bullet that struck his victim had missed the brain by a fraction of an inch, if it had been deflected inside the skull he would almost certainly have faced execution for murder – an ignominious end for a man who had gained a second lease of life as a fortunate survivor of the *Titanic*. Gaining remission, having served three years of his sentence, he was released from prison in 1937. Florence Hichen died of a brain tumour in March 1940 and her widowed husband did not survive her long. That summer he joined the crew of the cargo vessel *English Trader* and it was on this humble vessel that he suddenly fell ill suffering from fever and palpitations. He slipped into a coma and died onboard while the ship was off the coast of Aberdeen in September 1940. A post-mortem and the resultant inquest concluded that his death had been caused by heart disease.

During the year of Hichens' arrest in 1933, it had been widely reported that John Lee had died in Milwaukee, Wisconsin, where he had settled with former barmaid Adelina Gibbs after sailing to New York in February 1911. The reports of his demise proved to be groundless, although the

Horrified survivors watch the sinking of the *Titanic*.

convicted murderer did suffer a sad bereavement that year when his nineteen-year-old daughter Evelyn accidentally died through inhaling cleaning chemicals shortly after starting work as a domestic servant. International reports of John Lee's death had previously surfaced from Australia in 1918, Canada in 1921 and America in 1929, but he was to survive until April 1945. He passed away from heart failure at the age of eighty, having lived a full sixty years longer than he could possibly have expected when placed on the scaffold at Exeter Prison. Working until his retirement as a shipping clerk for a company manufacturing motor trucks, Lee avoided the glare of publicity associated with his infamous brush with the law and spent his days unaware of the extraordinary links forged by his criminal past to several other infamous crimes and murders of Devon.

BIBLIOGRAPHY & SOURCES

General Sources

Holgate, Mike and Waugh, Ian, *The Man They Could Not Hang*, Stroud, Sutton Publishing Ltd, 2005

Matthew, H.C.G. and Harris, Brian (eds) *Oxford Dictionary of National Biography*, Oxford, Oxford University Press, 2004

Website: www.wikipedia.org

Jack the Ripper: The Man Who Would be King

Ellis, Arthur, *Royal Occasions in Torquay*, Torquay, 1935

Finson, Robert, *My Story*, Exeter, 1817

Knight, Stephen, *Jack the Ripper: The Final Solution*, London, Grafton, 1977

Contemporary Journals: *Chicago Sunday Times Herald*, *Daily Northwestern* (USA), *Ilfracombe Chronicle*, *Leicester Mercury*, *The Times*

John Lee: The Man They Could Not Hang

Holgate, Mike, *Secret of the Babbacombe Murder*, Newton Abbot, Peninsula Press, 1995

Lee, John, *The Man They Could Not Hang*, London, C. Arthur Pearson, 1908

The Life and Trial of the Child Murderess Charlotte Winsor, London, Illustrated Police News, 1865

Contemporary Journals: *Dartmouth & Brixham Chronicle*, *East & South Devon Advertiser*, *Illustrated London News*, *News of the World*, *The Times*, *Torquay Directory & South Devon Journal*, *Torquay Times & South Devon Advertiser*

Patrick O'Donnell: The Man Who Avenged the Phoenix Park Murderers

Corfe, Thomas Howell, *The Phoenix Park Murders. Conflict, compromise and tragedy in Ireland 1879-1882*, London, Hodder & Houghton, 1968
Contemporary Journals: *The Freeman, Illustrated London News, The Times, Totnes Times & Gazette, United Ireland*

Oscar Wilde: The Man whose Love Dare not Speak its Name

Bentley, Joyce, *The Importance of Being Constance,* London, Hale, 1983
Hart-Davis, Rupert (ed), *More Letters of Oscar Wilde*, London, Murray, 1985
Hyde, Montgomery H., *Famous Trials 7: Oscar Wilde*, Harmondsworth, Middlesex, Penguin Books, 1962
Contemporary Journals: *The Theatre, The Times, Torquay Times & South Devon Advertiser*

Charles De Ville Wells: The Man who Broke the Bank at Monte Carlo

Contemporary Journals: *The Times, Thompson's Weekly News, Western Daily News*

Herbert Rowse Armstrong: The Man who Planned the Perfect Murder

Odell, Robin, *Exhumation of a Murder: The Life and Trial of Major Armstrong*, London, Harrap, 1975
Young, Filson (ed), *The Trial of Herbert Rowse Armstrong*, Edinburgh & London, William Hodge, 1927
Contemporary Journals: *Daily Chronicle, Daily Mail, Evening News, Mid Devon Advertiser, Sunday Chronicle, The Times*

Robert Hichens: The Man who Sank the *Titanic*

Baldwin, Jean, *The Book of Manaton*, Tiverton, Halsgrove Publishing, 1999
Lee, John, *The Man They Could Not Hang*, London, C. Arthur Pearson, 1908
Contemporary Journals: *Daily Mail, Herald & Express, Lloyd's Weekly News, New York Herald, Sunday Chronicle, The Times, Torquay Directory & South Devon Journal, Torquay Times & South Devon Advertiser*

Other local titles published by Tempus

Murder & Crime: Dover
JANET CAMERON

Those who fell foul of the law in Kent faced a horrible fate. This compelling book contains tales of thwarted rivals and wicked soldiers, desperate mothers, licentious monks and disreputable women. With more than fifty illustrations, this chilling catalogue of murderous misdeeds is bound to captivate anyone interested in the criminal history of the area.

978 07524 3978 5

Pirates of the West Country
E.T. FOX

Discover the handful of true West Country pirates of the past and also those that voyaged from the West to the Caribbean and Indian Ocean in this compelling history. These true tales of pirates operating from places such as Lulworth Cove, Plymouth Hoe and Corfe Castle inspired the pirate fiction we know today.

978 07524 4377 5

Haunted Devon
IAN ADDICOAT

From heart-stopping accounts of apparitions, manifestations and related supernatural phenomena to first-hand encounters with phantoms and spirits, this collection of stories contains new and well-known spooky tales from around the county of Devon. Compiled by the president of the Paranormal Research Organisation and drawing on historical, scientific and contemporary sources, *Haunted Devon* contains a chilling range of ghostly phenomena.

978 07524 3977 8

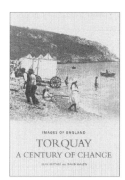

Torquay: A Century of Change
ALAN HEATHER AND DAVID MASON

Beginning more than 140 years ago, this book explores the style and grandeur of the town, the many fine villas and grand hotels built to accommodate the needs of the guests, the evolution of the railway and small villages surrounding the town, the seafront, the shops and traders, and the social occasions and café life of the 1920s and '30s.

978 07524 3960 0

If you are interested in purchasing other books published by Tempus, or in case you have difficulty finding any Tempus books in your local bookshop, you can also place orders directly through our website

www.tempus-publishing.com